# Boys'
## Underachievement in Education

AN EXPLORATION IN SELECTED
COMMONWEALTH COUNTRIES

By Jyotsna Jha and Fatimah Kelleher

Gender Section
Social Transformation Programmes Division
Commonwealth Secretariat
Marlborough House
Pall Mall, London SW1Y 5HX
United Kingdom
E-mail: gad@commonwealth.int
www.thecommonwealth.org/gender

Commonwealth of Learning
1055 West Hastings, Suite 1200
Vancouver, British Columbia
Canada V6E 2E9
E-mail: info@col.org
www.col.org

Publication editor: Tina Johnson
Cover and layout design: Alex Hennig
Printed by Ultratech Printing Ltd, Vancouver, Canada

Co-published by the Commonwealth Secretariat and the Commonwealth of Learning

Copies of this publication may be ordered direct from:
The Publications Manager
Communications and Public Affairs Division
Commonwealth Secretariat
Marlborough House
Pall Mall, London SW1Y 5HX
United Kingdom
Tel: +44 (0) 20 7747 6342
Fax: +44 (0) 20 7839 9081
E-mail: publications@commonwealth.int
www.thecommonwealth.org/publications

ISBN: 0-85092-845-1 / 978-0-85092-845-7

# Boys' Underachievement in Education

## AN EXPLORATION IN SELECTED COMMONWEALTH COUNTRIES

By Jyotsna Jha and Fatimah Kelleher

# ACKNOWLEDGEMENTS

Acknowledgements are due to:

Dr Tony Sewell (the lead consultant and coordinator of the case studies) and his team of researchers, including Ms Emma Charlton, Ms Pulane J Lefoka and Ms Elaine U Lameta for undertaking the research and preparation of the first set of reports.

Prof David Plummer, Prof Mark Figueroa and Ms Helena Fehr for providing helpful feedback on the first draft.

Ms Pauletta Chevannes for reviewing the Jamaican case study and providing useful information.

Ms Ann Keeling and Dr Henry Kaluba for their support and encouragement.

And all the others who contributed by providing information and preparing the final report.

# contents

## List of Figures

## List of Tables

# LIST OF ACRONYMS
# AND ABBREVIATIONS

| | |
|---|---|
| AARE | Australian Association for Research in Education |
| ACER | Australian Council for Educational Research |
| ADB | Asian Development Bank |
| AEU | Australian Education Union |
| BOCODOL | Botswana Centre for Distance and Open Learning |
| CARICOM | Caribbean Community |
| CCEM | Commonwealth Conference of Education Ministers |
| CFW | Change from Within |
| COL | Commonwealth of Learning |
| CSEC | Caribbean Secondary Education Certificate |
| CXC | Caribbean Examinations Council |
| DFID | Department for International Development, UK |
| EFA | Education for All |
| GDI | gender-related development index |
| GDP | gross domestic product |
| GER | gross enrolment ratio |
| GPI | gender parity index |
| HDI | human development index |
| ICT | information and communications technology |
| IRI | Interactive Radio Instruction |
| LDTC | Lesotho Distance Teaching Centre |
| LP | Learning Post |
| MDGs | Millennium Development Goals |
| MUSTER | Multi-Site Teacher Education Research Project |
| NAMCOL | Namibian College of Open Learning |
| NCNE | National Commission for Nomadic Education |

| | |
|---|---|
| NER | net enrolment ratio |
| ODL | open and distance learning |
| OECD | Organisation for Economic Cooperation and Development |
| OFSTED | Office for Standards in Education |
| PISA | Programme for International Student Assessment |
| PPSEAWA | Women for Peace, Understanding and Advancement |
| SACMEQ | Southern and Eastern Consortium for Monitoring Educational Quality |
| SLE | school life expectancy |
| SPELL | Samoa Primary Education Literacy Level |
| TES | Tertiary Entrance Score |
| TIMSS | Trends in International Mathematics and Science Study |
| UIS | UNESCO Institute for Statistics |
| UNDP | United Nations Development Programme |
| UNESCO | United Nations Educational, Scientific and Cultural Organization |
| UNICEF | United Nations Children's Fund |
| UPE | universal primary education |

# FOREWORD

The Commonwealth is a voluntary association of 53 States bound by a set of shared values and principles. One of those principles is that every child in the Commonwealth, girl or boy, has the right to a quality education. It will take some time for this right to be realised, however, since the majority of the 115 million children globally not in school live in Commonwealth countries. The majority of these children are girls. It is therefore right that the Commonwealth has focused attention on removing the barriers faced by girls in accessing education. More recently, however, Ministers of Education from across the Commonwealth have raised the issue of boys' underachievement and poor attendance at school, a growing phenomenon in all regions. This study, undertaken jointly by the Commonwealth of Learning and the Commonwealth Secretariat, responds to that concern.

The underachievement of boys in education is a subject that raises heated debate and a host of conflicting hypotheses. Three persistent myths surround the subject:

Myth one is that this is about 'boys versus girls'. It is not. The Millennium Development Goals (MDGs) agreed by all Commonwealth governments in 2000, commit States to eliminating gender disparities in education. That means addressing the needs of whichever gender – girls or boys – is falling behind in either access to education or achievement. We want therefore to understand and address boys' underachievement in education in the contexts where it is an issue whilst continuing to focus on girls' access to education elsewhere. It is not either one or the other. We are committed to doing both.

Myth two is that boys' underachievement results from 'a war of the sexes', and that somehow girls and maybe female teachers are responsible for boys falling behind. The roots of girls' exclusion from education lay in discrimination whereby girls in some places were banned from education, or more school places were provided for boys than girls. There is no such suggestion here that boys' underachievement is a result of any similar formal discrimination. In fact, this study argues that the same socially determined gender roles may impact negatively on both boys and girls. Both sexes can be victims of a culture that, for example, prescribes education as not 'cool' for boys and also tolerates violence against girls.

Myth three is that boys' achievement at school should be measured against that of girls. To further demonstrate that this is not a war of the sexes, both boys' and girls' achievement at school should be measured against objective education standards for all children at that stage of education. We are not saying, therefore, that boys are underachieving in education compared to their female classmates but that they are doing so against objective standards of literacy, numeracy, etc for their peer group.

A pan-Commonwealth study of boys' underachievement in education was an ambitious endeavour. Inevitably, there have been challenges concerning the availability and comparability of data. Inevitably also, given the diversity of the Commonwealth, there were differences in the social and educational contexts of the four case study countries. For example, the cattle herding duties that keep large numbers of boys out of school in Lesotho are unlikely to be a factor in Samoa. It is noteworthy, however, that despite the diversity of the countries it has been possible to identify common elements and trends.

It is generally accepted that a child's achievement at school will be determined by factors both inside and outside the school environment. The big question for many Ministries of Education will be what can be done inside the education system to improve the attendance and performance of boys. This study identifies examples of successful practice and initial recommendations for policy direction. Surprisingly, there were few examples of open and distance learning (ODL) strategies contributing to better performance in education by boys. This is an area COL will now pursue.

We believe this first Commonwealth policy study on boys' underachievement in education will spark important discussion at the 16th Conference of Commonwealth Education Ministers in Cape Town, December 2006. We anticipate that the issue will remain a significant one in our drive to ensure quality education for all in the Commonwealth and meet our shared commitment to eliminating gender disparities.

*Ann Keeling*
*Director*
*Social Transformation Programmes Division*
*Commonwealth Secretariat*

*Sir John Daniel*
*President & CEO*
*Commonwealth of Learning*

*October 2006*

# PART I: cross-country analysis

# 1.
# introduction and background

## THE ISSUE

Gender disparity in education is an old phenomenon. Traditionally, girls have been at a disadvantage in most parts of the globe, and they continue to be so even today. This is especially the case in the Commonwealth, where gender disparity is apparent in schooling participation rates in many countries. Although a number of Commonwealth countries in the Caribbean, Europe, East Asia and the Pacific have achieved gender parity in primary and even secondary enrolment rates, most Commonwealth countries in sub-Saharan Africa and South Asia still have significant gaps, with the proportion of girls not attending schools being much higher than that of boys. In fact, the Commonwealth is home to more than two thirds of the world's out-of-school children: nearly 75 million of about 115 million primary-school-age children in the world estimated to be not attending school. Girls have a disproportionate share, as about 35 to 40 million of the nearly 65 million girls out of primary school globally are in the Commonwealth.

*Gender disparity in education is an old phenomenon. Traditionally, girls have been at a disadvantage in most parts of the globe, and they continue to be so even today.*

However, a number of countries, many of them in the Commonwealth, have also made tremendous progress in girls' education in the last one to three decades. As a result, gender disparities are narrowing in many parts of the globe. At the same time, a new phenomenon has emerged in certain countries where gender disparities in education are turning in favour of girls, and therefore against boys, both in terms of participation and performance. This is particularly evident in countries that have achieved universal access and have high participation rates for both girls and boys, at least at the primary stage of schooling (including a number of Commonwealth countries in the Caribbean, Europe, East Asia and the Pacific, and some in sub-Saharan Africa and South Asia.

A commitment to achieving gender parity and equality in education in the Commonwealth makes it important to take note of this trend and to understand it better. This is the background leading to the present study, which was initiated as a response to this issue being raised by member countries at the 15th Commonwealth Conference of Education Ministers (CCEM) in Edinburgh in December 2003.

The fact that the entire debate on boys' underachievement views this in relation to the achievement of girls makes it look like a question of rivalry between boys and girls. Although it is unavoidable to compare the achievement of boys with that of girls in such a discussion, the framework used for the present analysis is not that of gender rivalry. On the contrary, this discussion views the issue as another manifestation of gendered social processes and uses the frame of gender equality to understand it.

The two aspects of boys' underachievement in education that will be considered are participation and performance, underachievement being used here as a relative term. This section initially focuses on participation followed by an analysis of trends in performance or learning outcomes at a later stage.

## Participation

Table 1 shows school life expectancy (SLE), representing the average number of years of schooling that individuals can expect to receive in different regions.

It is clear from the table that while SLE is higher for boys in sub-Saharan Africa, East Asia and the Pacific, and South and West Asia, it is higher for girls in Latin America and the Caribbean, North America and Western Europe. Both boys and girls experienced an improvement in SLE during 1998–2002 in all regions except for North America and Western Europe, which actually witnessed a decline in boys' SLE. However, the regions where SLE is higher for girls than boys are also the regions where SLE is higher for both boys and girls as compared to those where SLE is lower for both. Hence, though regional analysis has its limitations, as what is true for the region might not be true for all the countries therein, it can still be safely inferred that there is no uniform

TABLE 1: SCHOOL LIFE EXPECTANCY (SLE) BY REGION:
A GLOBAL PICTURE (2002 AND CHANGE SINCE 1998)

| REGIONS | SLE IN YEARS, 2002 | | | CHANGE (1998-2002) | | |
|---|---|---|---|---|---|---|
| | TOTAL | FEMALE | MALE | TOTAL | FEMALE | MALE |
| SUB-SAHARAN AFRICA | 7.8 | 7.0 | 8.5 | +1.1 | +1.0 | +1.1 |
| ARAB STATES | 10.2 | 9.6 | 10.7 | +0.4 | +0.5 | +0.2 |
| CENTRAL ASIA | 11.5 | 11.4 | 11.6 | +0.7 | +0.7 | +0.6 |
| EAST ASIA AND THE PACIFIC | 11.2 | 11.0 | 11.3 | +1.0 | +1.1 | +0.9 |
| SOUTH AND WEST ASIA | 9.1 | 8.4 | 9.7 | +0.6 | +1.0 | +0.3 |
| LATIN AMERICA AND THE CARIBBEAN | 13.1 | 13.3 | 12.8 | +1.0 | +1.1 | +0.7 |
| NORTH AMERICA AND WESTERN EUROPE | 16.4 | 17.0 | 15.3 | +0.2 | +0.4 | - 0.5 |
| CENTRAL AND EASTERN EUROPE | 12.8 | 12.8 | 12.8 | +1.0 | +1.0 | +0.9 |

Source: UNESCO, 2005.

pattern and that this trend of boys' under-participation is largely confined to areas that have experienced higher growth in educational attainment rates.

The absolute number of children adds another dimension to this phenomenon. The number of out-of-primary-school children, especially girls, is much higher in regions where SLE is lower for girls. Sub-Saharan African and South Asian Commonwealth countries fall in this category. It is interesting to note that the number of out-of-primary-school girls is higher than for boys even in Latin America and the Caribbean, where the SLE is estimated to be higher for girls. This means that the phenomenon of boys' under-participation concerns relatively smaller numbers and is not a major concern at the primary stage of education in any region (Table 2).

TABLE 2: NUMBER OF OUT-OF-PRIMARY-SCHOOL CHILDREN:
A GLOBAL PICTURE (1998 AND 2002)

| REGIONS | 1998 (IN THOUSANDS) | | | 2002 (IN THOUSANDS) | | |
|---|---|---|---|---|---|---|
| | TOTAL | FEMALE | MALE | TOTAL | FEMALE | MALE |
| SUB-SAHARAN AFRICA | 44,581 | 23,933 | 20,648 | 40,370 | 22,003 | 18,367 |
| ARAB STATES | 8,491 | 4,991 | 3,501 | 6,906 | 4,025 | 2,882 |
| CENTRAL ASIA | 775 | 400 | 375 | 635 | 341 | 294 |
| EAST ASIA AND THE PACIFIC | 8,309 | 4,151 | 4,158 | 14,782 | 7,372 | 7,410 |
| SOUTH AND WEST ASIA | 35,722 | 23,189 | 12,534 | 30,109 | 17,411 | 12,698 |
| LATIN AMERICA AND THE CARIBBEAN | 3,620 | 1,997 | 1,623 | 2,084 | 1,226 | 858 |
| NORTH AMERICA AND WESTERN EUROPE | 1,885 | 918 | 967 | 2,421 | 1,101 | 1,320 |
| CENTRAL AND EASTERN EUROPE | 3,340 | 1,830 | 1,510 | 2,569 | 1,366 | 1,203 |

Source: UNESCO, 2005.

The issue of boys' underachievement, however, assumes importance for later stages as evidenced in terms of lower transition and participation rates for boys in secondary and higher levels of education in many Commonwealth countries – not only in the Caribbean and the Pacific, but also in sub-Saharan Africa and Asia. Nevertheless, the analysis makes it apparent that lower transition rates from the primary to the secondary stage for boys in some countries might be a reflection of girls' low participation at the primary stage, and hence cannot be labelled as boys' underachievement. A lower net enrolment ratio (NER) for boys at the secondary stage, on the other hand, is a clearer indicator of gender disparity against boys for that level.

Table 3 selectively presents the picture from those Commonwealth countries that have reported either a higher transition rate from the basic to the secondary education stage or higher NER or both. The table does not include those Commonwealth countries, nearly 40 per cent of all, where both transition and NERs at the secondary stage are lower for girls. A perusal of the table indicates that the situation is quite varied even for these countries that show lower transition or enrolment ratios for boys. The diversity in the trend makes careful analysis and interpretation important.

A higher transition rate for girls in countries with a large disparity at primary level in favour of boys simply reflects a situation where a smaller percentage of girls reaches the final grade of primary, and hence a larger proportion continues to secondary, whereas a larger proportion of boys reaches the last grade and therefore a smaller proportion continues thereafter. In such situations, despite a higher transition rate, NER for girls remains lower than for boys at secondary level. Countries like India, The Gambia, Uganda and Zambia fall in this category. Boys' underachievement is therefore not an issue in such cases.

There is another set of countries where the transition rates are higher for boys but this still does not translate into higher participation rates at the secondary stage. This implies that a high level of drop out occurs for boys within the secondary stage. Then there are those countries where both transition rates and NER are higher for girls. Boys' under-participation is a concern in both of these circumstances. The countries in these two categories are also differentiated by the fact that the rates for boys' participation are lower than girls' in a situation of overall low enrolment rates in some countries (for example, a number of African and Asian countries such as Bangladesh, Lesotho, Namibia and Swaziland).

## TABLE 3: TRANSITION TO SECONDARY EDUCATION AND NET ENROLMENT RATIOS AT SECONDARY LEVEL IN SELECTED COMMONWEALTH COUNTRIES

| REGION AND COUNTRY | 2001-2002 TRANSITION RATE TO SECONDARY STAGE (%) | | | 2002-2003 NET ENROLMENT RATIO (NER) AT SECONDARY STAGE (%) | | |
|---|---|---|---|---|---|---|
| | TOTAL | FEMALE | MALE | TOTAL | FEMALE | MALE |
| **AFRICA** | | | | | | |
| BOTSWANA | 93.9 | 94.3 | 93.6 | 53.6 | 57.4 | 49.9 |
| GAMBIA, THE | 78.5 | 79.8 | 77.5 | 27.9 | 23.9 | 32.0 |
| LESOTHO | 66.9 | 66.7 | 67.0 | 22.5 | 27.2 | 17.8 |
| MAURITIUS | 62.7 | 68.4 | 57.4 | 74.4 | 74.5 | 74.3 |
| NAMIBIA | 83.3 | 85.2 | 81.2 | 44.2 | 49.7 | 38.7 |
| SEYCHELLES | 99.0 | 98.9 | 99.1 | 99.9 | 99.7 | 100.0 |
| SOUTH AFRICA | 91.9 | 93.0 | 90.7 | 65.5 | 68.4 | 62.7 |
| SWAZILAND | 78.1 | 79.6 | 76.6 | 32.4 | 35.6 | 29.3 |
| UGANDA | 42.2 | 44.1 | 40.7 | 16.5 | 15.6 | 17.4 |
| ZAMBIA | 54.5 | 55.6 | 53.5 | 22.2 | 20.6 | 24.9 |
| **CARIBBEAN** | | | | | | |
| BAHAMAS | 79.4 | 77.9 | 81.0 | 75.8 | 77.3 | 74.4 |
| DOMINICA | 96.5 | 97.4 | 95.8 | 91.8 | 97.8 | 86.0 |
| GUYANA | 67.6A | 70.7 | 64.7 | 76.4 | 77.9 | 75.0 |
| JAMAICA | 95.2B | 90.7 | 100.0 | 75.4 | 77.0 | 73.9 |
| ST LUCIA | 65.7 | 74.6 | 56.6 | 76.1 | 84.7 | 67.6 |
| ST VINCENT/GRENADINES | 51.1 | 57.8 | 44.2 | 58.4 | 60.8 | 55.9 |
| TRINIDAD & TOBAGO | 97.4B | 100.8 | 94.8 | 72.0 | 74.7 | 69.4 |
| **EAST ASIA AND PACIFIC** | | | | | | |
| AUSTRALIA | NA | | | 88.0 | 89.1 | 87.0 |
| FIJI | 98.4 | 96.6 | 100.0 | 76.0 | 78.7 | 73.4 |
| SAMOA | 97.5 | 99.4 | 95.7 | 62.1 | 65.4 | 59.1 |
| MALAYSIA | 99.7 | 99.5 | 100.0 | 70.0 | 73.8 | 66.4 |
| NEW ZEALAND | NA | | | 92.7 | 94.1 | 91.3 |
| TONGA | 78.9 | 77.6 | 80.1 | 71.1 | 76.7 | 67.5 |
| **EUROPE AND N. AMERICA** | | | | | | |
| MALTA | 90.7 | 92.0 | 89.6 | 86.8 | 87.8 | 85.8 |
| CANADA | NA | | | 97.6 | 97.9 | 97.4 |
| CYPRUS | 99.4 | 98.9 | 99.8 | 92.8 | 94.3 | 91.4 |
| UK | NA | | | 95.2 | 96.6 | 93.8 |
| **SOUTH ASIA** | | | | | | |
| BANGLADESH | 89.3 | 95.7 | 83.0 | 44.5 | 46.9 | 42.1 |
| INDIA | 86.7 | 89.0 | 84.9 | NA | | |
| SRI LANKA | 97.0 | 97.7 | 96.4 | NA | | |

A REFERS TO 1998-1999
B REFERS TO 2000 (UNESCO, 2004)

*Source: UNESCO, 2005.*

On the other hand, in some of the Caribbean and Pacific countries in the Commonwealth, the relative under-participation occurs in the context of overall high enrolment ratios.

## Performance

Underperformance of boys is another dimension of underachievement. It is not easy to assess performance and information is not readily available, especially such as would facilitate cross-country comparisons. Different learning outcome tests conducted in some countries are the major source of information. These include the Programme for International Student Assessment (PISA), the survey of the Southern and Eastern African Consortium for Monitoring Educational Quality (SACMEQ) and the Trends in International Mathematics and Science Study (TIMSS) being conducted in different groups of countries. Using these tests as the indicator for performance has limitations as learning outcome is only one aspect of performance. Moreover, the coverage of such tests has been limited to specific geographical areas. Nevertheless, they help to explicate certain significant aspects of educational outcome in those areas, and the available evidence shows the following important trends[1] :

- Girls tend to perform better than boys in countries where they have equal access to the school system, irrespective of the income level. In countries where girls are disadvantaged in terms of access, gender differences in achievement are generally small or insignificant, implying that girls do not usually underperform even when they are under-participating.
- Girls are usually more confident and perform better in reading as compared to boys. The gender differences are usually not high in performance in mathematics but girls feel less confident of performing well against boys.

## Understanding and addressing the issue

The above analysis establishes that though girls continue to be more disadvantaged in education and face inequalities in many ways, the emerging trend of boys' underachievement also needs attention, especially in terms of underperformance and in some cases even of under-participation. It is important to understand the nature and causes of the problem and look at the possible ways in which it could be addressed.

---

1    Based largely on trends as reported in UNESCO, 2005.

This study is based on the analysis of secondary data from various sources and case studies of specific examples conducted in four Commonwealth countries: Australia, Jamaica, Lesotho and Samoa. The conceptual framework used for the analysis is derived from the notion of gender equality in education as elaborated in the following section.

*... though girls continue to be more disadvantaged in education and face inequalities in many ways, the emerging trend of boys' underachievement also needs attention, especially in terms of underperformance and in some cases even of under-participation.*

# GENDER EQUALITY IN EDUCATION AND BOYS' UNDERACHIEVEMENT

Gender equality in education can be defined in several ways. Taking a cue from the capability approach, it can be defined as ensuring equality of entitlement, equality of opportunities and equality in the capacity to exercise the entitlements and use the opportunities for both girls and boys belonging to diverse social, ethnic, linguistic or economic groups. The notion of equality also refers to relational aspects and is linked to the issues of justice and freedom. Any practice or trend that prevents either boys or girls, or both, from realising their full potential to grow into responsible and aware individuals needs to be perceived as a hindrance.

Gender is a social construct, referring to the ways in which societies distinguish women and men and assign them social roles. Often mistakenly equated with the biological category of 'women', gender is actually a conceptual category referring to masculine and feminine qualities, behaviour patterns, roles and responsibilities. Femininity does not exist in isolation from masculinity as the construction and power of the one determines the construction and power of the other. This also leads to various forms of inequality and disparity between women and men that affect their capacities and lives in significant ways. It often works to the disadvantage of both: girls have to face restrictions and confinements in various forms; boys have to face the pressure of being breadwinners and protectors. It is in the interest of both men and women to move away from existing unequal relations of gender. Education can be and often is perceived as a process of expanding human capacities to contribute to the making of a just, equal and compassionate society. However, it is

*It is in the interest of both men and women to move away from existing unequal relations of gender. Education can be and often is perceived as a process of expanding human capacities to contribute to the making of a just, equal and compassionate society.*

not necessarily always a process of empowerment and transformation. It has equal potential or danger of being a process of socialising learners into existing norms, values and power structures and reinforcing unequal relations.

In this context, it is important to note that gender equality cannot be viewed in isolation from other forms of inequalities that exist in different societies. Societies are stratified in most parts of the world, and gendered differences often get sharpened by other dimensions such as race, ethnicity, location, class and other social or economic groupings that divide societies. Gender equality in education should encompass the issue of disparities and inequalities existing between different social and economic groups even within the same sex. Similarly, it should also encompass the diverse nature and extent of gender inequalities that exist within different groups.

The issue of boys' underachievement needs to be understood in light of the notion of gender equality as defined above. The questions that need to be addressed in this context are:

- What are the finer aspects of this phenomenon as they are seen in different countries?
- What are the variations in the nature of the trend as seen in different countries?
- What are the trends when it comes to specific social/ geographical/ ethnic groups in a particular country or region?
- Do socio-economic practices play any role in this and if so, what are these and how do they operate?
- How are these related to the socialisation process of boys and girls and to the expected gender roles in particular societies?
- How is this connected to curriculum and teaching-learning practices adopted in schools?
- Does this have any link with teachers' expectations, and if yes, what are these?
- Is there any difference in the level of motivation between girls and boys and, if so, what are the reasons?
- Do school and schooling processes question or reinforce the existing

societal norms of masculine and feminine behaviours, images and practices?

- How do these various factors, socio-economic backgrounds, socialisation, expected gender roles and schooling processes act on and interact with each other and get manifested in boys' underachievement?
- Does the trend of boys' underachievement mean a situation of gender privilege for girls?

Answers to these questions should help in understanding the trend, appreciating the underlying causes and developing various ways to address the issue.

# HOW THE REPORT IS STRUCTURED

The report is organised into two parts and seven chapters. In Part I, this introductory chapter is followed by a review of literature on the issue of boys' underachievement. The review helps in classifying the available literature on the basis of the arguments that have been used to explain the trend and therefore sets a context. The third chapter summarises the country case studies – from Australia, Jamaica, Lesotho and Samoa – and attempts to find answers to the questions posed above using both the available literature as well as the understanding emanating from the case studies. The discussion on the background of the identified countries also brings out their specific economic and social contexts. In addition, Chapter 3 points out to the limitations of this work and provides pointers for further research.

*A specific advantage that this study offers is that it is one of the first to provide a cross-regional analysis, as most existing studies have so far looked at the phenomenon in one specific context only.*

Part II contains the four country studies. The choice of countries from three different continents was determined by the desire to have regional representation of countries where the trend has been evident and that offer the potential to provide insights into the diverse nature of the issue. The case studies have largely focused on an in-depth understanding of one example of a school/ educational institution/ programme that has been perceived as a solution to the issue in the particular country. The interventions chosen include both formal and outside-formal[2] schooling initiatives, providing an insight into

---

2    The term 'non-formal' is being avoided deliberately as it has different connotations
     in education and is identified with particular programmes in various countries.

both kinds of strategies. The objective was to identify the commonalities as well as differences in the causes and the potential solutions to the issue of boys' underachievement.

A specific advantage that this study offers is that it is one of the first to provide a cross-regional analysis, as most existing studies have so far looked at the phenomenon in one specific context only.

# 2.
# what the existing literature says

## COMMON THEORIES
## AND PRACTICAL ANALYSES

It is important to note firstly that when speaking of boys' underachievement, much of the literature does so in a comparative context relative to girls' achievement in terms of indicators such as examination results, transitions to secondary school, repetition and adult literacy. This definition of underachievement has presented its own problems within the overall debate. Gorard, Salisbury and Rees (1999) challenge the methodologies used to produce calculations on achievement gaps in the United Kingdom between girls and boys. Acknowledging the problems around indices has led to recent literature including the term 'apparent underachievement' more often within the dialogue. This has been further informed as research has progressed to show that the statistics themselves – when disaggregated by other factors that go beyond the gender divide, such as region, ethnicity and parental income – show more complex results than a purely comparative approach between boys and girls would warrant.

*...the statistics themselves – when disaggregated by other factors that go beyond the gender divide, such as region, ethnicity and parental income – show more complex results than a purely comparative approach between boys and girls would warrant.*

The debate on boys' underachievement is not a new one in several Commonwealth countries. Discussed since the 1970s, it particularly came to the fore in the mid-1990s within the Commonwealth's developed countries of Australia, New Zealand and the United Kingdom. Debates on the matter were also gaining increasing focus in the Commonwealth

Caribbean. Outside of the Commonwealth, theories were being formulated in other countries such as Germany, Japan and the United States. These discussions were taken up at both popular and academic levels, and the period has since been viewed as one of "moral panic" around the incidence of boys' underachieving (Gorard, Salisbury and Rees, 1999). As noted by Epstein et al (1998), discussions prominent at the time need to be understood within their historical context. They outline the existence of material that goes back to the 1970s on working class boys' alienation from middle class schooling values, and also look at the prevailing arguments debated at the time: 'pity the poor boys' – which attributed boys' underachievement to 'lost control' and rising feminism; 'failing schools failing boys' – which challenged school effectiveness in the provision of education for boys; and 'boys will be boys' – which tackled the issue from an essentialist position of inherent differences of gender compatibility with schooling.

In sub-Saharan Africa, although there have been reports from some countries of boys' underachieving (which seems to be largely tied to drop-out rates rather than to poor performance), the continued problem of girls' lack of access and resultant academic underachievement means that the literature is still very much in its infancy. Similarly, despite recent reports from some Commonwealth countries in the Asia-Pacific region of boys' underachievement, literature on relevant countries has been difficult to locate except from Australia and New Zealand. Assuming that the literature on these areas is in fact scant, this suggests either that the phenomenon is very new or that the issue has so far stayed away from both the journalistic and academic radars.

Out of the plethora of these inter-locking arguments, backlashes and already existing reviews on the literature, this chapter seeks to locate the most common strands within the material available on Commonwealth countries. As noted, the literature on the situation in Australia, New Zealand and the United Kingdom is substantial. At the policy level also this issue has been thoroughly addressed in these countries. In Australia, an inquiry into the issue led to a report called *Boys: Getting it Right* (House of Representatives, Standing Committee on Education and Training, 2002), while the New Zealand Education Review Office produced a publication on the *Achievement of Boys* (Aitken, 1999). In the UK, the Office for Standards in Education published *The Gender Divide: Performance*

*Differences Between Boys and Girls at School* (OFSTED, 1996), which focused primarily on the increasing visibility of boys' lower exam scores than girls'. The debates in these countries have resulted in the rise of programmes targeted at increasing boys' achievement levels. This is true in the Caribbean as well, where the Jamaican Government, for example, conducted a study and developed programmes in response to its findings to address issues such as adolescent disaffection.

Theoretically, there has been a strong focus on masculinity within gender identity. These theories have evolved significantly over the last decade, going from the 'poor boys' and 'boys will be boys' arguments that couched much of the discussion within the framework of disadvantage (due to disaffection from increasingly girl-centred school systems), towards calls for an acknowledgement of multiple masculinities within society and the classroom context, and the recognition of further societal factors affecting results-based underachievement. Within the overall approach of masculinity studies, there are various sub-sections that present themselves quite clearly for analysis.

Further theoretical considerations that take into account the interplay of socio-economic factors and gender identity are also prevalent. The authors of these writings put much of their analysis within situational contexts that allow the discourse on boys' underachievement in general to be unpacked by asking more specifically: which boys? This has allowed in-country specificities to be more deeply analysed. Pulled from this broad topic are three key, integrated themes that have recurred regularly within the literature across several Commonwealth countries: economic disadvantage and class; ethnicity and language; and economic alignments within gender roles. An additional area of research that has emerged in this context relates to school processes. A case study of an Australian school (Lingard et al, 2002) falls in this category. The same school was revisited by the present research, and the case study on Australia presented later in the report looks at the observations made by Lingard et al in detail. Since not many case studies discuss school processes as a separate causal aspect of boys' underachievement, this review looks at the issue only within other contexts of gender identity and masculinity.

# GENDER IDENTITY: DEBATING MASCULINITY

Concepts of the impact of masculinity on boys' performance have been popular throughout the debate on boys' underachievement. Studies that tackle the impact of gender stereotyping and set values of masculinity within society and the classroom are found throughout the available literature. The Caribbean experience in particular has been tackled from this standpoint. A study conducted by CARICOM and the University of the West Indies (Bailey and Bernard, 2003) shows strong indicators towards boys' academic underachievement in terms of performance and drop-out rates. Figueroa (2000), in his study on male academic underachievement in the English-speaking Caribbean, starts with the premise that male underachievement is an ironic outcome of male privileging: men have traditionally occupied a wider social space in Caribbean history, but are now the victims of this privilege as women "carve out for themselves spaces which they hegemonise and within which the freedom of the privileged group is restricted". This "dialectic of privilege" is also referred to by Davis (2002), who argues that the problem of boys' underachievement in Trinidad and Tobago, "like in other cultural contexts", is defined by the issues of "historical privilege, gender socialisation, masculine expectations and how schools are organised for learning".

*Concepts of the impact of masculinity on boys' performance have been popular throughout the debate on boys' underachievement.*

The definition of masculinity itself has proved problematic for academics tackling this issue, and has been caught between dominant, popular perceptions of masculinity within societies on the one hand and a reality of multiple masculinities on the other. Davis (2002) tackles the plurality of masculinity that often arises by simply putting forward "the social and culturally constructed meanings or definitions attributed to being male" as a working definition and, although he also argues that masculinity should be considered in multiple forms, he maintains that the "traditional" or "conservative" perspective of masculinity usually dominates the discourse. In addressing the developing literature on masculinities, West (1999) looks at the portrayal of masculinity in the media using clichés that depict masculinity as natural and innate, and he suggests that there has been slow progress in the academic study of the subject that would more clearly highlight the term's multiplicity. The public debate, he further argues, dominates the academic one, a consequence of the issues around boys' underachievement being linked to feminism, and any questioning of boys' perceived difficulties being linked with a "reaction against feminism". Addressing "common themes of masculinity", West's study unpacks "traditional" masculinity as being based on three dicta – perform, protect, provide – that incorporate the idea of proving and testing (proving to/ testing by other men, women, themselves) that "they are not female". This dialogue often takes place around and through the male body, with a focus on measurements through physical strength, and is informed through mediums such as Hollywood in the most simplistic of terms.

The focus of a traditional 'maleness' as the antithesis of femininity has (perhaps inevitably) provided ample material on sexuality within gender stereotyping and the prevalence of homophobic underpinnings within traditional concepts of masculinity. This argument is one explored by Figueroa (2000) as a consequence of schooling being perceived by Jamaican boys as a feminine endeavour and, in a society where homophobia is prevalent within the music and popular culture, male bookishness running the risk of accusations of homosexuality. More generically, West (2002) presents the bleak view that "when you are a 14-year-old boy, almost anything can be called gay if it does not endorse Neanderthal masculinity". Epstein (1998) addresses the problem within the context of school bullying and the resultant negotiation by boys, whether heterosexual or gay, around dominant heterosexist expectations in the classroom.

## Gender roles and the 'feminisation of academia'

Popular in the writing on the impact of traditional masculine identities on boys' underachievement is the perceived femininity of studies by boys. Figueroa (2000) starts by placing this area within the Jamaican context and argues that female gender roles are more conducive to the requirements of successful studious behaviour. He contends that girls' early childhood socialisation and their role within the household work well with the demands of homework and reading, whereas the social space occupied by boys rejects this. As equal opportunities have increased within the educational system, these female gender identities have become more and more in tune with the ethos of education (discipline, more adult supervision, more responsibility) while boys have increasingly been alienated from inhabiting the space of academic aspiration. As boys fall behind within schooling, this problem becomes exacerbated by their acquisition of a defensive posture that translates into negative associations such as homophobia.

Some of the literature on the feminisation of schooling has a complexity that places it within the limits of (a) certain academic subjects that are dominated by girls, often referred to as 'soft' subjects; and (b) a certain time-frame of schooling that sees these perceptions of femininity being overcome by some boys as they grow older. This presents a broader perspective on the overall issue of boys' academic underachievement that challenges the idea of boys being disadvantaged in the long term. However, the literature also provides dissenters to these standpoints.

The humanities and languages in particular have come under serious focus as the areas where boys mainly underachieve. Marks (2001) shows that by age 14 girls in the UK start to substantially out-perform boys in English. Boys' lower performance has been attributed to the use of more 'female-oriented' reading materials, with suggestions that the inclusion of more factual, 'male-oriented' works could increase male performance. This argument can also be found in Hunte (2002) in the context of Guyana.

*A number of studies... have pointed out how better performance by boys in traditionally feminine subjects such as languages is perceived to be 'gender inappropriate' and hence undesirable in different contexts.*

A number of studies have pointed out how better performance by boys in traditionally feminine subjects such as languages is perceived to be 'gender inappropriate' and hence undesirable in different contexts. Figueroa (2000) ties this discussion into a broader issue of Creole and slang and their usage by boys in Jamaican society as a badge of masculinity, whereas standard English is viewed as effeminate. This issue surrounding language presents a further dialogue on class and ethnicity that will be explored later. More generally, Figueroa (2000) once again approaches the dominance of better female performance in the humanities as a consequence of gender stereotyping, where 'harder' subjects, such as the physical sciences and mathematics, continue to be the preserve of males. In the Guyanese context, Hunte (2002) argues the opposite by maintaining that as time goes by, the sciences are also becoming more open to women. The changing roles of men and women, he argues, are proving to be educationally disadvantageous for men, with "the educated male fast becoming an 'endangered species'", as witnessed by the outnumbering of men by women at the tertiary level graduations of the University of the West Indies and the University of Guyana.

Conversely, in one of the few findings on this subject in Africa, the Multi-Site Teacher Education Research Project (MUSTER) included statistics showing that despite successful attempts to address gender stereotyping in Lesotho – with boys showing considerable interest in such traditional female subjects as nutrition and cookery – there was nonetheless a rise in drop-out rates among boys as they reached late primary and transitioned to early secondary school (Jobo et al, 2001). This has linkages with economic issues, discussed later.

Epstein's study (1998) on British education draws attention to the limitations of the timeframe within which the impact of masculine perceptions and the subsequent view of schooling as 'feminine' takes place. She argues that although girls outperform boys in schools from late primary up to the taking of GCSE examinations, this phenomenon does not extend to the sixth form and 'A' levels, where boys become free to aspire academically due to a shift within masculine identity from anti-'feminine' and anti-school, to that of a "muscular intellectualness" inherent within hegemonic middle-class masculinity. But the fact that the British sixth form is a non-compulsory form of education, coupled with the availability of this "muscular intellectualness" in only a narrow class context, presents further questions of socio-economic factors and academic universality that need to be addressed when studying boys' underachievement. In other words, while disaffection towards schools may inhabit a limited timeframe, and any disparity for middle-class boys may be redressed in later stages of academia, educational opportunities would already have passed for many boys who lack the privileges of class.

## Male role models

The absence of male role models is a factor that comes up regularly within the literature on boys' underachievement, and it assumes the stance that boys' needs within both school and the broader society are different from those of girls. In the Caribbean context, where the number of women-dominated and single-parent households has been on the rise, the literature reviewed presents strong concerns about the lack of male presence within the home as well as the school. Hunte (2002), in the context of Guyana, argues that boys will seek out negative macho role models to fill the gaps at home or school, and that the resultant anti-schooling attitudes will leave an emotional deficit that inhibits their progress. Figueroa (2000) takes this further and suggests that the absence of discipline meted out to boys in Jamaica by women – who believe this to be the preserve of a father or other male figure – disadvantages boys by permitting their exploration of negative masculine identity to be played out unchecked.

West (2002) analyses the problem of an imbalance of male and female teachers, which potentially disadvantages boys by giving messages that 'only women teach' and 'only women read'. His paper further outlines studies that have been conducted in Australia showing that boys value male teachers as role models to get them through the difficulties of the classroom. West quotes a paper by Bress (2000), who argues that males and females have a different language – 'genderlects'. This theory arguably takes the issue of role models out of purely socialisation discourses and into the more contentious area of gendered heredity. One of the few findings that addressed the issue of boys' educational underachievement and under-participation in Lesotho also stressed the lack of male teachers in the educational system. However, the MUSTER project conducted in that country showed that the cause of boys' dropping out was more often in order to fulfil work obligations due to hard economic circumstances (Jobo et al, 2001).

The literature surrounding male role models, especially in relation to the Commonwealth's developed countries, also has an ethnic dimension. For example, a wealth of literature on the underachievement of Afro-Caribbean boys in the UK educational system presents nuances that go beyond simply gendered responses. Parallels with the United States, where disaffection towards school among African-American boys has also dominated the literature, are common. The academic literature in the UK concentrates heavily on issues of 'institutionalised racism' such as teacher expectations, streaming and curriculum relevancy. The call for black male mentors is often heard within popular debate on the subject at the operational grassroots level and in the media. A similar situation can be evidenced in Australia, where the underachievement of Aboriginal and Torres Strait Islander boys is assessed by Aboriginal workers, as reported in the *Boys in School Bulletin*, as being partly due to there being very few Indigenous men employed in high educational positions (2000a). Another issue that comes up in the same article is the inability of non-Indigenous teachers to address specific cultural issues. Interestingly, despite records of low achievement by white working-class boys, the literature is not as overwhelming in its call for role models drawn from that class of society.

> *The absence of male role models is a factor that comes up regularly within the literature on boys' underachievement, and it assumes the stance that boys' needs within both school and the broader society are different from those of girls.*

## Teacher expectations

Some authors have argued that teachers in the classroom have been guilty of gender stereotyping, and that low expectations of boys' behaviour and academic effectiveness contribute to the levels of boys' underachievement. Figueroa (2000), for example, suggests that there is a growing ambivalence within the Jamaican educational system that allows the misbehaviour of boys to continue, partly as a result of reluctance to curb the tendencies of traditional masculinity that would endanger that identity. Davis (2002) goes further to argue that boys are treated differently than girls as early as pre-school, and that throughout primary school they receive lower ratings by teachers for social behaviour and academic expectations. Martino and Berrill (2003) put forward work suggesting that male teachers in particular sometimes reinforce gender stereotypical behaviours in boys rather than challenging them.

*Some authors have argued that teachers in the classroom have been guilty of gender stereotyping, and that low expectations of boys' behaviour and academic effectiveness contribute to the levels of boys' underachievement.*

Jones and Myhill (2004a) argue that the identity of the underachiever has become synonymous with the stereotypical identity of boys. What is interesting is the authors' concern that such teacher expectations are not based on a belief of boys' innate academic inability, but more a belief in boys' innate inclination to misbehave despite being quite bright, often due to boredom. These teachers run the risk of rendering girls invisible and of attributing girls' higher achievement purely to hard work and performance, whereas boys are seen as harbouring natural but latent abilities. In another study, Jones and Myhill (2004b) articulate this concern further by suggesting that when teachers attribute high performance to girls as a gender norm, the underachieving girls become overlooked, whereas the high-achieving boy is credited for having challenged his gender stereotyping.

## Single sex or co-education?

The debate over whether boys perform better in single-sex or co-educational schools remains fractured. Arguments that suggest boys adopt anti-school masculine identities as a response to the feminised ethos of schooling can lend themselves to conclusions that the provision of single-sex schools might be effective in alleviating the problem. Hunte (2002) argues that, in Guyana's case, the re-introduction of single-sex secondary schools could put the education of boys on a fast track, as such schools are able to bring boys' emotional and learning needs more sharply into focus. Davis (2002) claims that single-sex school will allow the freedom of multiple masculinities, but also maintains that although these schools can help boys to embrace the diversity of male roles, many position themselves as restoring a "normative masculinity" and act as compensatory institutions.

Research conducted in New Zealand has provided evidence that boys in single-sex schools perform better than boys in co-educational schools. The Education Review Office report (Aitken, 1999) showed that both boys and girls achieved better results in single-sex schools. Interestingly, however, even though boys in single-sex schools outperformed both boys and girls in co-educational schools, they lagged even more significantly behind their female counterparts in single-sex schools than they would have done their female counterparts in co-ed schools. Further data provided by the report also suggested higher levels of managerial performance from girls' schools as opposed to boys' schools. This, together with the continued higher academic performance levels of girls over boys in single-sex schools, fosters the earlier arguments that girls and schools are somehow conducive to one another where boys and schools are not. But the statistics offered by this report also disaggregate the overall percentage finding according to other factors such as the rural-urban divide and public-private school ownership. These data present marked contrasts in the levels of underachievement among boys, suggesting that deeper reasons going beyond the gender divide are also at play.

# THE INTERACTION OF SOCIO-ECONOMIC FACTORS AND GENDER

Reed (1998) argues for the social justice perspective when dealing with the education of boys and maintains that, by focusing simply on the "distribution of goods" (i.e., qualifications), the dialogue is ignoring other important factors such as structural inequalities, institutional processes and the separation of the private from the public sphere. This article focuses primarily on the performance of schools and boys' underachievement, but the issues tie in with broader concerns, such as social class, economic under-privilege, poverty and ethnicity. Epstein et al (1998) clearly state that "overall, the 'underachievement' of boys at school is a strongly classed and racialised phenomenon", and that class and parents' education continue to be the most reliable indicators of a child's educational attainment. Nyland (2001) goes one step further to include residential address as an indicator, and argues that educational reform needs to go deeper than changes to curriculum and pre-service teaching courses. The earliest literature that focused on masculinity and gender identity had a tendency to make vague references to some of these issues. More recently, however, authors have moved towards analysing the interface between the masculinity debate and other factors that have allowed boys to be more accurately viewed in smaller groups. This has enabled the literature to reflect the diverse factors that can affect different groups of boys towards academic underachievement, and present a clearer picture of the complex causes behind the phenomenon.

## Economics, class and gender identity

While many of the problems that arise from class and economic disadvantage within the findings are also entwined with the more detailed debate on ethnicity, a distinction is being made for the sake of recognising the two as related but distinct factors. UNICEF (2004) outlines the role that poverty has to play in boys' underachievement in the Caribbean and Latin America, where governments have become increasingly aware that boys and young men are more likely to be alienated from school if they come from poor socio-economic backgrounds. A DFID study in Botswana and Ghana also shows the relationship between economic disadvantages and boys' underperformance (Dunne, 2005). Although Botswana is ahead of Ghana in terms of universal primary education (UPE) and educational provision for girls, overall statistics in the study showed boys achieving more than girls. This pattern, however, went into reverse in Ghana in the poorest peri-urban and rural schools that also registered the lowest scores overall. In those areas, better relative performance by girls could be seen. In Botswana there were two case studies where girls out-performed their male counterparts, and again these were in the poor, low-achieving schools.

Across the globe in New Zealand (and across the development line as well), statistics in the report by the Education Review Office (Aitkin, 1999) also show that the underachievement of rural boys relative to rural girls is far greater than that of urban boys to urban girls. In this instance, the study points to the limited options available in rural schools and the lack of opportunity to study specialist subjects, but no specific mention is made of socio-economic disadvantage. A possible contributory factor put forward by the DFID study for the Botswana and Ghana case studies was the lower attendance rates of boys in schools within the peri-urban and rural areas (Dunne, 2005). The study identifies reasons for boys dropping out in those areas of Ghana as related to employment opportunities.

However, although the literature above has outlined that it is common to see the most underachieving boys coming from socio-economically disadvantageous backgrounds, the literature also maintains the fact that girls in those groups are still out-performing their male social counterparts. So although both sexes may be adversely affected by these circumstances, and therefore both achieve below those from higher social classes, boys nonetheless remain at the bottom of even this more detailed hierarchy. This is corroborated by Brown (2001) in the case of Jamaica, where the suggestion is that boys are affected differently by economic and class issues within the society, such as the tendency towards engagement in crime. Figueroa (2000) explains that the minority of boys who do very well in school in Jamaica start their education within the privilege of the private prep school.

*...it is common to see the most underachieving boys coming from socio-economically disadvantageous backgrounds...*

These lines of arguments that show economic disadvantage being related to the adoption of certain types of masculine identity ultimately lead to a conclusion by some authors (such as West, 1999) that anti-school manifestations of traditional masculinity are more commonly found among working-class boys. Mahoney (1998) recommends that more work needs to be done on how boys from UK working-class backgrounds are "subordinated by the practices, values and conceits of white, middle-class modes of masculinity".

## Ethnicity, language and gender identity

Mahoney's usage of not just 'middle class' but also 'white' brings us to the next socio-economic sub-factor that has received considerable attention in the literature. Within the discourse of poverty, economic disadvantage and class there exists a further one on the roles of ethnicity and language within boys' underachievement. Much of the data on this has come from developed countries in the Commonwealth where racial and ethnic polarities and their relationship to the economic power structure already feature significantly in broader academic discourses. In the UK, this refers mainly to the Afro-Caribbean community, but also to others where low academic achievement is particularly evident, such as among Bangladeshi and Turkish boys. Mortimore (1988) noted the relationship between economic disadvantage, class and ethnicity in London's schools. Much of the literature on Australia in this regard refers to Aboriginal and Torres Strait Islander boys, while lower levels of achievement have been noted in New Zealand among the children of immigrants from the Pacific Islands as well as the Maori community.

A wealth of literature, going back decades, exists on Afro-Caribbean boys underachieving within the British education system. The focus on boys, however, is often seen within the much broader context of underachievement by both girls and boys in those communities. Coard (1971) was one of the first to critique the UK education system for being unresponsive to the needs of black children and for inherent institutional racisms. Graham and Robinson (2004) used a methodology where black boys voiced their own experiences. The authors argue that British educational policies continue to deny the existence of race and racism and to consider the different positioning of black boys in the wider society. Richardson (2005) has edited an anthology of work that tackles the underachievement of black children. One of the interesting points to come out of this book is in relation to the debate on 'tiering' within exams, and how negative expectations by teachers of black children, and in particular of boys, result in attainment ceilings being placed above them.

Much of the popular debate about black boys' underachievement has revolved around the assumption that the group operates as a homogenous disaffected entity. Explanations can lean easily towards 'blameist' arguments, with the influence of rap music, absent fathers and gun violence being held directly responsible. Indeed, when debating disadvantageous socio-economic circumstances, even when also addressing institutional racism that refuses to acknowledge these circumstances, some of the heterogeneity that exists within the group can be overlooked. Moving beyond the Commonwealth for examples, we see much of the data produced on underachievement of socially disadvantaged (and often black) boys in Brazil is related to the call of street culture and gang peer pressure. Sewell (1998) sought to address differing attitudes among underachieving Afro-Caribbean boys through empirical research at an inner-city school in the UK. His findings placed the boys within categories that were defined by differing characteristics, such as "conformists" and "retreatists", as well as "rebels". He concludes, contrary to much of the literature that has been produced, that the school constructs a more complex, ambivalent and contradictory male identity, with many boys actually positioning themselves within a pro-school stance.

In Australian research, both West (1999) and Nyland (2001) indicate the prevalence of underachievement from Aboriginal and Torres Strait Islander boys. West highlights that especially at risk are Aboriginal boys and boys from homes where the first language is not English. Nyland adds children with learning difficulties and those living in isolated rural areas, but more specifically takes up the impact of home language on achievement. She argues that where the Australian school curriculum expects language to be used appropriately, the term 'language' actually simply means English.

*Much of the popular debate about black boys' underachievement has revolved around the assumption that the group operates as a homogenous disaffected entity.*

But these broader dynamics of power and inequality again do not adequately explain why boys from these marginalised groups in Australia continue to achieve less than their female minority counterparts. This was more adequately approached in the Jamaican context by Figueroa's (2000) explanation mentioned earlier of the perceived femininity of standard English and the masculine association with Creole and slang, particularly among boys from poorer backgrounds. In that context, the interface between economic disadvantage, gender identity and ethnicity as it pertains to the use of language is arguably clearer. One of the many discrepancies that come up within the Australian literature in terms of ethnicity is the relative 'over achievement' of boys who come from Asian cultural backgrounds. Similarly in the UK, this applies to students of Indian origin (although with the underachievement of Bangladeshi boys, the South Asian grouping is also fractured in this respect) and East Asian boys.

New Zealand has also produced material on the underperformance of Maori boys relative to their white counterparts. While the Education Review Office report (Aitkin, 1999) mentions Maori boys only in the context of schools where boys have performed better, the *Boys in Schools Bulletin* (2000b) provides evidence of consistent underachievement by both Maori boys and more broadly by boys deemed to be of a low economic status. There is also evidence to suggest that Pacific Island children living in New Zealand fall within that bracket.

What is also clear in all these cases is that while boys' underachievement within those social groups is a problem, girls in those groups are also underperforming in relation to their female counterparts from higher status social groups. In many cases they also under-perform against boys from higher status social groups. This phenomenon is seen clearly in the UK among many minorities. A Report of Education Scrutiny Panel (2003) into the underachievement of Turkish boys concluded with recommendations that while the panel was formed to investigate boys, the major cause of the underachievement – low rate of English language acquisition – affected both sexes. What it did not clearly outline were the differentials in achievement between Turkish boys and girls.

## Cultural economic alignments with gender roles

Of the less abundant literature available from Africa where boys are not academically achieving as well as girls, the alignment of gender and economic roles emerges more clearly as a determinant of boys' dropping out of school and underachieving. The DFID comparison between Botswana and Ghana already mentioned highlighted the lower performance of boys relational to girls within peri-urban and rural schools, and attributed this in part to the need for those boys to access employment opportunities at an earlier age (Dunne, 2005). Further research on Botswana noted in *Equals Newsletter* makes a correlation between the traditional role of boys as cattle herders and increased drop-out and low enrolment rates in the transition from primary to secondary school (Challender, 2004). The absence of fathers and older brothers, who leave to work in the diamond mines, puts the pressure on boys to take on this position. With half of families in Botswana owning cattle, this is not necessarily a factor only applicable to economically marginalised groups. A 'graduation' on to the mines as the boys grow older only compounds the perceived lack of need for boys' education. Within this scenario, as the Newsletter clearly notes, there is a complex issue of macroeconomic policy (an undiversified economy reliant on natural resources) and a new slant on traditional gender roles from those we have so far encountered in the literature in Australia, New Zealand, the UK and the Caribbean (ibid).

*What is also evident in all these cases is that while boys' underachievement within those [minority] social groups is a problem, girls in those groups are also underperforming in relation to their female counterparts from higher status social groups.*

Similarly, the MUSTER paper on Lesotho places that country's current experience with boys' underachieving in school within an economic and cultural history of gendered economic alignment (Jobo et al, 2001). It argues that male child labour is very common in Lesotho, with young boys in the rural areas being denied their right to education by being hired out as herdboys from a very young age. This phenomenon is rooted in Lesotho's past, where boys from 18 years of age would go the South African mines and parents felt that boys did not need any education to work. The retrenchment of more and more men from the mines has yet to be adequately addressed within this attitudinal standpoint. And yet, despite the lack of education of many boys in Lesotho in comparison to their female counterparts, the MUSTER paper also points out that women are still significantly discriminated against in other spheres of life (ibid).

## BOYS UNDERACHIEVEMENT IN THE WIDER GENDER EQUITY CONTEXT

This leads to the consideration of a further strain within some of the literature that has been produced on boys' underachievement, which essentially seeks to answer the question: Where should one place the debate around boys' relative underachievement in school within the wider context of overall gender equity? As Epstein (1998) notes, the mid-1990s movement towards boys' issues initially produced a 'the future is female' fear as part of the panic that resulted from evidence of boys' apparent underachievement in school. Jackson (1998) notes that in the UK "the language of educational inequality has dramatically shifted over the last twenty years", from the focus on girls' disadvantage in the 1970s, to the mid-1990s when boys' disadvantage took centre stage. The debate on boys and school became grounded in a to-and-fro scenario between anti-feminist backlashes and counter-backlashes. In the Caribbean, we have already seen in the work of Hunte (2002) that boys are being viewed as an "endangered species" as a result of their educational underperformance.

Yet, some of the literature places the debate within equity indicators outside of strictly educational attainment. In Lesotho, for example, as noted above, female educational achievement was shown not to equate with increased socio-economic progress (Jobo et al, 2001). Women were still legally regarded as minors, with very little economic power such as land ownership. And this paradox is not restricted only to an arguably extreme case such as Lesotho. Although not all the studies on the Caribbean concur with this, Figueroa

(2000) clearly highlights evidence that suggests women have to gain much better qualifications than their male counterparts in order to access the work market, with men still achieving far more in the employment sector despite their overall lower grades. By positioning his debate about boys' underachievement as inseparable from various forms of "patriarchal capitalist restructurings", Mahoney (1998) argues that there is a danger that discussions on transforming masculinities, even from the most radical stance, can overlook the secondary positioning of women within the wider spectrum of gender relations.

Although such considerations are increasingly mentioned in much of the literature, there has been a lack of more inclusive research into the cumulative positions of men and women in society. Broader indicators such as economic ownership, political participation and relative earnings according to gender have not fully been put into context on this issue of boys' underachievement relative to girls even by those countries mentioned in this chapter that have yielded the most literature.

*Broader indicators such as economic ownership, political participation and relative earnings according to gender have not fully been put into context on this issue of boys' underachievement relative to girls...*

This review of literature, along with the conceptual frame outlined in the first chapter, provides the context for analysing the issue of boys' underachievement by going deeper into the trends in four Commonwealth countries: Australia, Jamaica, Lesotho and Samoa. The case studies of different initiatives in these four countries are analysed in the next chapter to understand the phenomenon better and trace pointers for policy or programmatic solutions. The chapter also attempts to identify areas for further research in this context.

# 3.
# varying dimensions and lessons emerging from selected commonwealth countries

This chapter attempts to broaden the existing understanding of boys' underachievement by looking at the situation in four Commonwealth countries – Australia, Jamaica, Lesotho and Samoa – in greater depth. The analysis is primarily based on the case studies of these countries found in Part II, but it also draws from the existing literature wherever relevant. For each of these four countries, it tries to identify the causes for the issues as they exist in that context and analyses an initiative undertaken to address the situation in order to determine (a) how far this has succeeded in the specific context, and (b) to what extent it has the potential for providing indications for policy or programmatic solutions.

## SOCIAL AND ECONOMIC BACKGROUND OF THE COUNTRIES

The four countries that were identified for this study are different from each other not only in terms of size and location but also in a number of social and economic indicators, as demonstrated by Table 4.

## TABLE 4: SELECTED DEVELOPMENT INDICATORS FOR AUSTRALIA, JAMAICA, LESOTHO AND SAMOA

|  | AUSTRALIA | JAMAICA | LESOTHO | SAMOA |
|---|---|---|---|---|
| INCOME CATEGORY | HIGH | LOWER-MIDDLE | LOW | LOWER-MIDDLE |
| POPULATION (MILLIONS) | 20.1 | 2.7 | 0.8 | 0.2 |
| PER CAPITA GDP (US$) | 29,632 | 4,104 | 2,561 | 5,854 |
| HUMAN DEVELOPMENT INDEX (HDI) | 0.955 (3) | 0.738 (98) | 0.497 (149) | 0.776 (74) |
| GENDER-RELATED DEVELOPMENT INDEX (GDI) | 0.954 (2) | 0.736 (75) | 0.487 (114) | NA |

Notes:
1. HDI is a composite index based on life expectancy at birth, adult literacy rate, combined enrolment ratio for primary, secondary and tertiary education and per-capita gross domestic product (GDP).
2. GDI is based on life expectancy, education index and income index.
3. Figures in parentheses in Rows 3 and 4 represent the respective world ranking.

*Sources: Income category from the World Bank, 2006; other information from UNDP, 2005.*

While Australia is a large country with a population of more than 20 million, Lesotho and Samoa are tiny in comparison, each with a population of less than a million, and Jamaica is also comparatively small with a population of less than 3 million. A large proportion of the Australian population is made up of immigrants from diverse backgrounds and a small proportion consists of aboriginals, who are now marginalised in social and economic terms. The society has a multicultural nature, and different languages are spoken at home. It is a high-income country with a high level of human development and gender equality, yet it has pockets of inequalities in terms of socio-economic development as well as education.

Lesotho, a landlocked African country, and Samoa, a country consisting of two large and six small islands in the Pacific, are relatively homogenous in terms of the nature of their populations and languages. Lesotho is a low-income country with a low rank in human development and gender equality as measured by the *Human Development Report* (UNDP, 2005). A third of the population lives in the highlands and most people speak Sesotho. Livestock forms an important part of their lives. Samoa has a single system of societal organisation and language. Economically, it is much more advanced than Lesotho, the per capita GDP in the former being more than twice as high as the latter.

Jamaica is closer to Samoa in economic and developments indicators. Both are lower-middle income countries falling somewhere in the middle in the human development and gender equality world rankings. The most populous English-

*...these four countries... provide a diverse picture of social features and economic development, therefore presenting an opportunity to understand the commonalities as well as the varying nature of the phenomenon of boys' underachievement in different contexts.*

speaking Caribbean island, Jamaica is a predominantly black nation, with approximately 98 per cent of the population being of total (90.9 per cent) or partial (7.3 per cent) African descent. The remainder of the population is made up of East Indians (1.3 per cent), Chinese (0.2 per cent, whites (0.2 per cent) and 'other' (0.1 per cent).[3] Although racial differences are not as important as class differences, the lightness of one's skin is still an issue, especially since the minorities are generally members of the upper classes.

It is obvious that these four countries in the Commonwealth provide a diverse picture of social features and economic development, therefore presenting an opportunity to understand the commonalities as well as the varying nature of the phenomenon of boys' underachievement in different contexts.

# THE ISSUE: COMMONALITIES AND DIVERGENCES

The preceding chapters have highlighted that

i   the issue of boys' underachievement in education is essentially viewed and discussed in relative terms, contrasted to the achievement of girls in education, and

ii  underachievement in education has two dimensions: under-participation and underperformance.

This section looks at these two dimensions of boys' underachievement in relation to girls' in the four countries, as depicted by the various available indicators. While it is relatively easy to get information on participation indicators for different countries that are comparable, this is always not the case with performance indicators. Countries adopt different ways of assessing performance, and information on these is not readily available. Hence, for participation an attempt has been made to use comparable indicators using the same data sources, whereas for performance whatever data is available for

---

3   Jamaican information on population from 2006 CIA World Factbook: *www.cia.gov/cia/publications/factbook/fields/2075.html.*

different countries has been accessed and analysed. Despite these limitations of data, the analysis provides an idea of the situation in these countries in a comparative sense.

## Relative under-participation of boys in schooling

A perusal of Table 5 shows that the situation in terms of literacy and educational participation at school level is quite different in these four countries.

TABLE 5: SELECTED EDUCATIONAL INDICATORS FOR
AUSTRALIA, JAMAICA, LESOTHO AND SAMOA (PERCENTAGES)

|  | AUSTRALIA | JAMAICA | LESOTHO | SAMOA |
|---|---|---|---|---|
| ADULT LITERACY RATE (MALE) | NA | 79.8 | 73.7 | 98.9 |
| ADULT LITERACY RATE (FEMALE) | NA | 80.2 | 90.3 | 98.4 |
| GENDER PARITY INDEX (GPI) IN LITERACY RATE (FEMALES/ MALES) |  | 1.00 | 1.22 | 1.00 |
| NET ENROLMENT RATIO (NER) – PRIMARY (MALE) | 96.4 | 94.4 | 82.9 | 98.6 |
| NER – PRIMARY (FEMALE) | 97.2 | 94.8 | 88.6 | 96.4 |
| GPI IN NER – PRIMARY (FEMALES/ MALES) | 1.01 | 1.00 | 1.07 | 0.98 |
| NER – SECONDARY (MALE) | 87.0 | 73.9 | 17.8 | 59.1 |
| NER – SECONDARY (FEMALE) | 89.1 | 77.0 | 27.2 | 65.4 |
| GPI IN NER – SECONDARY (FEMALES/ MALES) | 1.02 | 1.04 | 1.53 | 1.11 |

*Source: UNESCO, 2005.*

Australia is a fully literate (not shown in the table) country with a high level of participation by both boys and girls at both primary and secondary levels. Participation is not universal, however, and more needs to be done to raise enrolment rates at the secondary level. Gender parity is slightly tilted in favour of girls at both primary and secondary levels, but the disparity is marginal and therefore not significant.

Samoa is close to Australia in terms of literacy at higher than 98 per cent for both males and females, with a GPI of one (showing complete gender parity). The enrolment ratios for primary education are also high and similar to those of Australia, but the same is not the case for secondary education where enrolment ratios are much lower. Gender parity is in favour of boys at primary level but it changes sharply at secondary level. Not only do girls have a much higher enrolment ratio, but the differences between the enrolment ratios are also much higher in comparison to those at primary level. This trend occurs while the enrolment ratios for both boys and girls remain low in general, and lower in comparison to Australia.

Jamaica presents a picture somewhat similar to Samoa in terms of enrolment ratios. At primary level these are nearly 95 per cent for both boys and girls, but gender disparity occurs at secondary level where the enrolment ratio for boys is lower than that for girls. The level of difference between boys and girls, however, is less than that for Samoa at secondary level as participation remains high for both sexes in Jamaica. On the other hand, the literacy rate in Jamaica is much lower at only about 80 per cent for both males and females. Lesotho, which is economically much behind Jamaica, has a significantly higher literacy rate for females. However, it is the only country out of these four that shows significant gender disparity in literacy rates, relatively lower yet quite notable disparity in primary level participation rates and very high disparity in secondary level enrolment ratios.

*The...analysis makes it clear that under-participation is a major issue for boys in Lesotho; it starts at primary level and becomes very serious at secondary level.*

The above analysis makes it clear that under-participation is a major issue for boys in Lesotho; it starts at primary level and becomes very serious at secondary level. However, this disparity needs to be viewed in a situation of very low levels of participation for both boys and girls at secondary level. Under-participation is also an issue in Samoa at secondary level, while that is not the case for the primary stage of schooling. Jamaica falls in the same category as Samoa, though the level of under-participation is not as high as Samoa even at secondary stage. Australia does not appear to be facing the problem of under-participation of boys at any level.

## Relative underperformance of boys in schooling

### Australia

The major issue relating to boys' underachievement in Australia is underperformance. Two types of sources have been used to indicate this: secondary stage results and the outcomes of Programme for International Student Assessment (PISA), a large sample survey in Organisation for Economic Cooperation and Development (OECD) countries and a few developing countries. A number of indicators for secondary stage education in the 1990s indicated underperformance of boys in different parts of the country. For example, aggregate results at Grade 12 level show that in the 1999 New South Wales Higher School Certificate, for subjects studied by more than 100 students, the girls' average mark was higher than the boys' in 36 of the 40 subjects by up to 11 per cent. In 1998 in Queensland a greater proportion of girls were in the top performance bands in 36 of 45 Year 12 subjects, and in 1998 in South Australia a higher proportion of girls were in the top performance bands in 27 of 34 subjects in Year 12. The difference between boys' and girls' average results in the New South Wales Tertiary Entrance Score (TES) widened from 0.6 marks in 1981 to 19.4 marks in 1996, with the difference increasingly rapidly in the early 1990s.

Australia was one of the top scorers in all three areas – reading, mathematics and scientific literacy – in the PISA 2000 results. No significant difference in girls' and boys' performance in mathematics and science was reported in any of the Australian states or territories in 2000. PISA 2003 also did not show any gender difference in the means for overall mathematical literacy in Australia. But twice as many males as females achieved the highest PISA proficiency level, showing that girls were at a disadvantage when it came to mathematics. The situation changes, however, when it comes to reading literacy. Girls performed better than boys, though the level of difference was lower in Australia than most other OECD countries. The gap also varied between different states and territories within the country, being significantly higher in some as compared to others.

The Australian analysis also shows that socio-economic status compounds the difference between boys and girls in the case of reading literacy. Boys from low socio-economic backgrounds were found to be almost twice as likely to be in the lowest quarter of reading literacy results as girls from similar backgrounds. The results for mathematics and science also show a relationship between socio-economic status and the likelihood of achieving a low score, but this is the same for both boys and girls in science and not large enough to be significant in mathematics. Thus the relationship between socio-economic status and achievement in mathematical and scientific literacy in Australia was not as strong as the relationship for reading literacy. This suggests that schools may play a larger role in the development of mathematics and science skills than they do in reading skills, a conclusion that is corroborated by the fact that students in Australia who came from a non-English-speaking home background performed at an equivalent level in mathematical literacy to students whose home language was English, but at a lower level in reading and scientific literacy.

Students' results also showed some differences according to the location of their schools. Students in provincial cities performed as well as students in large cities and major urban areas, but students whose schools were in remote areas performed worse than other students in reading and scientific literacy. There was no difference in mathematical literacy results by location of school. The environment outside school appears to be having an important role in building reading literacy and to some extent scientific literacy.

An analysis of results related to 'engagement with reading' provides some insights into girls' higher reading literacy scores. 'Engagement with reading' reflects how much students like reading, how much they enjoy talking about books and going to libraries, whether reading is a favourite hobby, and so on. Australian students were at the same level as the OECD average in this area, but girls scored significantly higher than boys on this index in most countries including Australia. Attitudes towards reading were moderately strongly related to reading achievement in Australia.

*... gender is only one dimension of differentiation that characterises the performance outcomes of 15-year-olds in Australia. Socio-economic status turns out to be more critical for both boys and girls.*

It is also noteworthy that though nearly 40 per cent of Indigenous students in Australia performed on par with the average, in general they performed at a lower level than the non-Indigenous students in all three assessment areas. Gender differences were similar to the other Australian students, with females outperforming the males in reading literacy. No significant gender differences were found in mathematical or scientific literacy.

The analysis of PISA results makes it clear that gender is only one dimension of differentiation that characterises the performance outcomes of 15-year-olds in Australia. Socio-economic status turns out to be more critical for both boys and girls. However, what makes gender important is that similar trends of no significant difference in mathematics and science scores and a significant difference in favour of girls in reading literacy are observed for all socio-economic and social groups.

### Jamaica

A study on gender differentials in enrolment and performance at the secondary and tertiary levels undertaken by the Caribbean Community (CARICOM) has been used as the major source for getting evidence for performance-related indicators in Jamaica (Bailey and Bernard, 2003). Using data submitted by countries for the June 2002 Caribbean Secondary Education Certificate (CSEC) examinations offered by the Caribbean Examinations Council (CXC), it was able to determine male/ female achievement gaps by subjects.

The CARICOM study shows that boys' and girls' achievements in Jamaica are evenly distributed at the General Proficiency level in 11 science subjects, with each gender having an achievement gap advantage in five subjects and one subject showing no evident advantage either way. The trends are somewhat similar to Australia, as girls perform relatively better in languages and the humanities and boys in science and mathematics. In the humanities (General Proficiency) girls clearly show better performance in all the subjects with the exception of French. With English language and literature being included in this category, the concerns regarding diminished literacy among boys and therefore the lack of rudimentary capacities needed for further education and learning are clear. Jamaica thus faces both under-participation and underperformance of boys at the secondary level of schooling.

## Lesotho

Lesotho does not show a clear trend of boys' underperformance. The results of the second round of Southern and Eastern Consortium for Monitoring Educational Quality (known as SACMEQ II), an assessment survey held in a number of African countries, has been used here as a source. SAQMEC originated from a survey in Zimbabwe in 1991 and was later expanded to 13 countries, which included Lesotho in the second round. SACMEQ II assessed reading and mathematics achievements of Grade 6 on a sample basis. Boys and girls showed similar scores in almost all areas of Lesotho in these tests. The results of SACMEQ II 2000-2002 show that there is no notable difference between boys and girls even in reading literacy in the country. This is despite the fact that repetition rates are higher for boys. According to a report by the Ministry of Education and Training (2000), girls perform better than boys in all the grades at the primary education level, but the scores for both sexes level off in the final examinations. The main problem with boy's underachievement in Lesotho is under-participation.

## Samoa

Two kinds of indicators are used for understanding performance in Samoa. The country has a system of conducting tests at the end of Years 4 and 6 in three subject areas: English, Samoan and numeracy. These assessments are used as diagnostic tests to identify low scorers, with those not achieving a minimum level of desired competencies being designated 'at risk'. This is one source of information for lower levels. Another is the mean scores achieved in different subjects at the end of Years 8 and 12. Admission to post-basic level after Year 8 is determined by performance in the National Year 8 Examination, and hence it assumes special significance even for participation at the secondary stage of schooling.

The results for different years show that the proportion of boys identified as being 'at risk' has consistently been higher than that of girls for all three subject areas for both Years 4 and 6. The proportion of those not achieving the minimum desired competencies increases for both boys and girls in English and numeracy and decreases for Samoan at Year 6 in comparison to Year 4, but the disparity between the sexes continues, the proportion 'at risk' being much higher for boys in all the subjects. Unlike other countries, boys are not performing better even in numeracy in Samoa. In other words, with about 69 per cent of boys and 44 per cent of girls being 'at risk' in English and 76 per cent of boys and 58 per cent of girls being 'at risk' in numeracy (Government of Samoa, 2004a), the situation is alarming for both sexes, though far worse for boys.

A perusal of mean scores achieved in five subject areas – basic science, English, mathematics, Samoan and social sciences – for the National Year 8 Examination at the end of the primary level for 2001, 2002 and 2003 clearly show girls as performing better than boys in all subjects. The trends are similar for Year 12 results, where girls outperform boys in terms of mean scores in all subjects including mathematics, economics and physics. The difference, however, in mean scores is less notable in physics and mathematics as compared to other subjects such as economics, English or Samoan. Chemistry is the only subject where boys show consistently higher mean scores than girls for the period (2001-2004) for which data have been analysed. Although mean scores can be a deceptive indicator (as they do not reveal the proportion that actually achieves the mean, below mean or above mean), they do indicate clearly that boys are underperforming in Samoa. There is under-participation as well as underperformance, the former being more notable at secondary level while the latter is an issue at both primary and secondary levels. Underperformance at primary level could be one of the causes leading to under-participation at secondary level.

*Summary*

The above analysis makes it clear that Australia and Lesotho each face one aspect of boys' underachievement in education: Australia faces only underperformance whereas Lesotho faces only under-participation. On the other hand, Jamaica and Samoa face both under-participation and underperformance, especially at secondary level. The problem is sharper and more obvious in Samoa as compared to Jamaica. Boys' underperformance is limited to languages and humanities in Australia and Jamaica, which is the trend in most other countries wherever boys' underachievement has been noticed, whereas this is visible for almost all subjects in Samoa. The following section discusses some of the reasons that could explain these findings.

# WHAT EXPLAINS THESE TRENDS?

This section draws from the country cases as well as from the available literature on boys' underachievement, gender equality and masculinities from these countries and elsewhere in and outside the Commonwealth. An effort has been made to understand these issues in their particular contexts by identifying general as well as typical causes of the trends in boys' underachievement as reflected through various means and measures. The analysis shows that, while it is important to understand the specific context, certain underlying causes are fairly universal. This is especially so in the case of boys' underperformance, particularly in languages and the humanities. Under-participation, on the other hand, has a range of explanations, some having similarities while others are very context specific.

In this regard, it should be stressed that boys' underachievement in any of these countries is not a result of the secondary position of men or gender under-privileging, and hence cannot be compared with the under-participation in education that girls have faced in all parts of the world at some point in time, and continue to face in many places even now. Most societies are primarily patriarchal and, despite varying degrees of change witnessed over time,

*... it should be stressed that boys' underachievement in any of these countries is not a result of the secondary position of men or gender under-privileging, and hence cannot be compared with the under-participation in education that girls have faced in all parts of the world...*

gender relations remain in favour of men in more than one way. For instance, Lesotho's patrilineal and patriarchal system continues to subordinate women to men, and the customary law classifies women as minors that need to be perpetually subjected to the guardianship of their male counterparts. Customary laws and tradition also remain paramount in Samoa. The *aiga*, or extended family, is important in terms of decisions and is headed by *matai*. While women are not prohibited by the Constitution from being elected as *matai*, many villages ban women for being chosen for this position. This restricts their political participation as only *matai* title holders can run for elections. In general, customary law and tradition provide greater power and authority to men (PPSEAWA, 2004). The data from these four countries on economic and political participation, the two major indicators for women's empowerment, clearly reveal that even where the law does not differentiate between the sexes, women's participation rates are visibly lower than those of men (Table 6).

TABLE 6: ECONOMIC AND POLITICAL PARTICIPATION OF WOMEN IN AUSTRALIA, JAMAICA, LESOTHO AND SAMOA: SELECTED INDICATORS

|  | AUSTRALIA | JAMAICA | LESOTHO | SAMOA |
|---|---|---|---|---|
| FEMALE ECONOMIC ACTIVITY (%), 2003 | 56.7 | 67.3 | 47.7 | NA |
| FEMALE ECONOMIC ACTIVITY AS % OF MALE RATE, 2003 | 79.0 | 86.0 | 56.0 | NA |
| % SEATS IN PARLIAMENT HELD BY WOMEN, 2005 | 24.7 | 11.7 | 11.7 | 6.1 |
| % WOMEN IN GOVERNMENT AT MINISTERIAL LEVEL | 20.0 | 17.6 | 27.8 | 7.7 |

*Source: UNDP, 2005.*

This indicates that the explanations for boys' underachievement either in terms of under-participation or underperformance in education have to be located within a situation where men continue to be advantaged in terms of power and privileges. The apparent reasons as emanating from different sources and case studies have been classified into three categories:

i   social, economic and occupational practices;

ii  paucity of school places and facilities; and

iii conformity to 'masculine' gender identity and 'feminisation' of schools.

## i. Social, economic and occupational practices

Some socio-economic and occupational practices appear to play a role in keeping boys away from schooling, especially in Lesotho, and to some extent in Jamaica and Samoa.

As noted earlier, the highlands in Lesotho, where about one third of the population lives, have a tradition of boys herding livestock. Apart from being a source of pride, these animals are an important source of livelihood, and wealth was traditionally counted in terms of the number of livestock a family had. From as early as the age of ten, herdboys spend their days taking the family's livestock to a field where they can graze. During winter this often means taking the animals a few miles from home; when spring planting begins, these young boys need to move the herd further up into the mountains to look for pasturelands. Herdboys are one of the main groups that remain outside the fold of modern education. A number of researchers have pointed out that herding of animals is considered a good practice even in terms of socialising the male child to become a responsible member of family and society (Mokhosi et al, 1999). Most herdboys come from a poor family background, and the situation is worse for children who serve other families as herdboys and stay with their employers. They work for poor remuneration from a tender age and are denied many basic rights.

*Some socio-economic and occupational practices appear to play a role in keeping boys away from schooling, especially in Lesotho, and to some extent in Jamaica and Samoa.*

A clear relationship to socio-economic or occupational practices is less obvious in Jamaica and Samoa. In Jamaica, women have a higher unemployment rate despite having higher educational participation and achievement rates. For instance, unemployment rates for males in 2004 stood at 8.1 per cent as against 15.7 per cent for women, and in terms of active job-seeking only 4.5 per cent of males were looking for work as against 8.4 per cent of women.[4] It is possible that the labour market favours male employment and as such women continue with higher education as the only available choice. Women may also need to perform better to compete with men in a market that shows a bias towards male employment. However, in the absence of clear evidence, these are only conjectures.

The employment data in Samoa reveals that a high proportion of men are employed in traditional occupations such as agriculture, hunting and forestry,

---

4    Data from Statistical Institute of Jamaica, Jamaican Labour Force Statistics. Available at: *http://www.statinja.com/stats.html*

the proportion being as high as 44 per cent as against 14 per cent for females according to the 2001 national census (Government of Samoa, 2003c). It is likely that a preponderance of occupations that do not call for modern education as a pre-requisite means there is no catalyst to increase the demand for secondary schooling among males. However, there is no definite evidence to arrive at this inference conclusively. It is also possible to surmise that the labour market favours male employment and therefore women have to have higher qualifications to compete, and as such they continue their studies while boys discontinue theirs.

## ii. Paucity of school places and facilities

A deficit in the supply of schools, school places and adequate schooling facilities appears to be playing an important role in boys' underachievement in Lesotho and Samoa. Highland areas in Lesotho face a paucity of teachers, especially qualified ones, as lack of facilities makes rural areas unattractive. A study undertaken by the Government of Lesotho and the World Bank (2005) revealed that 51 per cent of teachers in mountain areas are unqualified, compared with only 24 per cent in lowland areas. Even these figures may mask greater teacher shortages in the most isolated schools, many of which might not have any or only one qualified teacher.

Samoa appears to be facing the problem of a lack of school places at secondary level. Admission to secondary schools depends on performance in Year 8 examinations, and underperformance of boys at primary level translates into under-participation at secondary level. Therefore, though the paucity of school places is not directly responsible for boys' underachievement, an increase would enable more boys and girls to participate in secondary schooling. This is perhaps particularly true for rural areas as there is a concentration of facilities in the major island. Available information from Australia and Jamaica does not show any such trend.

It is important to add at this juncture that a paucity of qualified teachers or school places should affect both boys and girls, and it is difficult to assert that it affects boys more adversely. However, when seen in conjunction with the prevalent practice of boys adopting the profession of herdboy in Lesotho, and with an admission policy based on Year 8 results in Samoa where boys are underperforming, it can be safely inferred that such deficits affect boys' participation more adversely in these specific situations.

## iii. Conformity to 'masculine' gender identity and 'feminisation' of schools

Conformity to 'masculine' gender identity that clashes with the demands of so-called 'feminised' education emerges as the most important and common reason given to explain underperformance of boys in general, and in humanities and reading in particular. While this relationship is clearer and better researched in Australia and Jamaica in comparison to Lesotho and Samoa, the evidences of 'masculine' identities and expectations of conformity to these are clear even in those two countries. What is not so obvious in these two cases is how this relates to the underachievement of boys.

*Conformity to 'masculine' gender identity that clashes with the demands of so-called 'feminised' education emerges as the most important and common reason given to explain underperformance of boys...*

There are several dimensions of differentiated gender identity that interact with education and provide certain explanations for boys' underachievement. As mentioned earlier, gender is a social construct, referring to the ways in which societies distinguish women and men and assign them social roles. Every society has its own notions of feminine and masculine qualities, behaviour patterns and roles and responsibilities. Despite minor and sometimes major differences in these notions across different societies, certain aspects of what define masculinity and femininity appear to be fairly universal. Men are universally viewed as warriors and protectors and women as care-givers. Masculinity is associated with physical and mental toughness, the capacity to conceal emotion, capability for sexual conquest and fatherhood, and with not being feminine. 'Not being feminine' assumes special importance when one tries to trace the relationship between masculinity and boy's underachievement in education (see chapter 2).

Formal education started as a male prerogative, and women across different parts of the globe earned this right only after much struggle over time. Till a few decades ago, education was still men's preserve even in the Western world. For girls and women, it was a special accomplishment to be able to access and complete education. With the rise of the feminist movement and the struggle for equal rights for women, having equal access to education became an important goal as well as a means for women's advancement. Education has been and is seen as a means of attaining other rights for women, and education itself is viewed as an achievement. As such, one of the factors that explain the better performance of girls is the sense of accomplishment that is attached to education for women.

However, the societal notions of masculinity and femininity have entered the arena of education as well. The streams of education and the professions that were considered most 'suitable' for women had their roots in the care-giving role and included subjects such as home-science, teaching, languages and nursing. Masculinity, on the other hand, came to be associated with subjects that demanded either precision or 'application of mind', e.g., science, mathematics and economics, or physical strength and power such as sports. Having equal access to and opportunities for education in all subjects and entry to all professions, including so-called 'masculine' ones, is something that women are still fighting for across the world. Therefore, an important distinction that came into being is that entry to traditionally 'men's subjects' or 'men's professions' is an achievement for girls and women, but the opposite is not the case for boys and men. Since masculinity continues to be associated with 'not being feminine', anything that is considered 'feminine' is considered not 'masculine' enough.

The socialisation of boys also affects their personalities, perceptions and performance in education. A perusal of the literature on masculinity in the context of homophobia emanating largely from countries like Australia, Jamaica, the UK and the US helps illuminate the nature of homophobic references, its impact on the masculine identity of boys and its relationship with boys' underperformance in education. Plummer (1999), for instance, traced through research in Australia how the use of words with homophobic connotations starts early at primary stage and targets boys for many non-sexual behaviours and preferences as well. A number of these words are used, among other things, against boys who prefer academic pursuits or solo men's sports over team sports, who are interested in reading books and doing well in class, who are 'teacher's favourite' or who choose subjects that are 'feminine' and so on. These have deeply negative connotations and serious implications for boys' behaviour and personality.

Plummer (2003) rightly argues that

> [during] crucial early periods in a boy's development homophobic words are deployed against non-sexual targets and these meanings persist into adulthood alongside later antigay connotations. Coherence between the early (nonsexual) and later (antigay) meanings is achieved because all of the meanings (early and late) share the quality of targeting behaviours and characteristics that are deemed inappropriate for boys as they mature. Thus homophobia is rooted in gender dynamics, but rather than specifically marking the inter-gender divide

between masculinity and femininity, homophobia marks an intra-gender divide between appropriate, peer-endorsed masculine behaviour and a lack of appropriate masculinity (a failure to measure up).

Conformity to peer-endorsed masculine behaviour in school has direct implications for their performance, especially in languages and reading. Plummer (2005) suggests that "while not inherently gendered, the discourses deployed by the boys reveal that these transgressions do have a gendered basis…homophobia is triggered by departures from the expectations of the male peer group: by doing anything that, according to the group, a 'real man' would not do".

Seen from this perspective of what is referred to as 'hegemonic masculinity' by some[5], school and education are viewed as 'feminised'. Boys are not supposed to have an academic orientation and should not have any allegiance to teachers, as it would be tantamount to betrayal of the peer perception of 'manhood'. The fact that a particular kind of language that promotes use of slang is considered appropriate for boys, as discussed in the last chapter in the context of Jamaica, makes it difficult for them to perform well in language. On the other hand, as noted earlier, the feminisation argument also stems from the fact that girls' early childhood socialisation and their role within the household works well with the demands of homework and reading (Figueroa, 2000) and suits the ethos of education. It is obvious that the way these notions affect boys' performance is complex and multilayered. On one hand, inter-gender divides play a role where girls come to school with a different kind of socialisation, making them more amenable to schooling processes and demands; on the other, intra-gender pressures further push boys away from academics, especially certain subjects.

In this context, it is important to point out that the debate on masculinities and their impact on boys' underachievement also helps in understanding the class or racial/ ethnic characteristic of the phenomenon. The review of literature in the previous chapter has shown how in the context of Australia, Jamaica and the UK, boys from working-class backgrounds are more likely to continue with anti-school manifestations of masculinity, drawing them towards crime and anti-social behaviour in their adulthood, whereas boys from middle-class backgrounds find an alternative manifestation of masculine identity in the form of intellectual pursuits.[6]

*On one hand, inter-gender divides play a role where girls come to school with a different kind of socialisation, making them more amenable to schooling processes and demands; on the other, intra-gender pressures further push boys away from academics, especially certain subjects.*

---

5   See Connell (1987).
6   See, for instance, Epstein (1998), Figueroa (2000), Brown (2001), West (1999, 2002) and Mahony (1998).

# THE INITIATIVES

The case studies from Australia, Jamaica, Lesotho and Samoa that form the next four chapters have tried to document the experiences of certain initiatives at micro level. Two of these are formal schools while the other two are outside the formal primary or secondary education system. In their own way, all of them have tried to address the issue of boys' underachievement, and the analysis of the experiences offers some lessons. This section provides a summary of the interventions followed by a discussion of the lessons learnt for (and questions raised about) likely solutions to the issue.

## I. Creating a learning organisation in a multicultural, poor socio-economic neighbourhood, Australia

The school that was identified for this case study was a government inner city co-educational primary school located in Queensland. The school had previously been the subject of a detailed case study and identified as "one of the best for boys" by Lingard et al (2002), and the conclusions drawn in this case study are based on the earlier observations as well as those made in a recent visit.

A large primary school located in a low-income area, with over 800 students and 65 teachers, the school faces multiple challenges because of the socio-economic and linguistic background of its students. Most of the children's families are poor, coming from various cultural backgrounds and ethnic/linguistic minorities. Student absenteeism has been high, late arrival common and behaviour management a major issue. The school is especially relevant to this report because

   i   socio-economic status is the most important factor related to underperformance of students in Australia;

   ii  boys relative underperformance is evidenced largely in reading literacy; and

   iii  the difference between boys and girls achievement outcomes for reading literacy is wider for lower socio-economic status groups.

The school has been maintaining a database of progress of students, which shows positive change over the years. The school considers its focus on a collaborative pedagogical approach as the key to its success. This approach is said to help everyone, both those who have traditionally been underachievers and those who have been performing well. The reasons for this success can be traced to imaginative and committed leadership from the principal and a number of pedagogical reforms initiated in the school. Strategies for greater involvement of parents have also been introduced.

The analysis of the experiences of this school helps in identifying two specific practices that has helped the school and its children perform well:

i   An empathetic understanding of the socio-economic, linguistic and cultural background of students; and

ii  A focus on cooperation and engagement in teaching methods and learning opportunities.

Interviews with both teachers and the principal showed that they recognised the challenges of the poor socio-economic status and multicultural backgrounds of students, but that they also saw this as an opportunity. Most teachers showed a good understanding of students' backgrounds and the impact these could have on behaviour as well as learning, and none of the students interviewed shared any negative experience from any teacher in this context. There was an overall belief in children's innate desire and ability to learn, with the principal noting that it is schools or individuals that switch off this basic desire.

*The school considers its focus on a collaborative pedagogical approach as the key to its success.*

The school focuses on cooperation and teamwork in its pedagogy and the kinds of learning opportunities it tries to create. It uses double teaching spaces, and two teachers work as a team to teach two grades. The use of interactive whiteboards in all double classroom spaces is a special feature of the school and provides a good example of the potential that technology has in making classrooms more engaging and interactive for students. Classroom observations showed that children enjoyed taking turns on the board and discovering new aspects of whatever they were learning through its use. Students also mentioned how, in addition to making subjects more interesting, using the board helped them to develop skills such as teamwork and sharing. Special efforts are made to engage children needing special attention. No gender differentiation was observed in terms of work allocation and efforts to engage children in different activities.

Interviews with teachers, students and the principal as well as classroom observations suggested that the school did not have any specific intervention for boys or girls, and did not perceive this to be a major issue. Rather, the teachers were addressing the needs of each child depending on her or his situation. Students did not perceive of subjects as 'feminine' or 'masculine', as was seen in some of the statements they made in their interviews when several boys identified the arts as their favourite subject. When they did express stereotypical notions about boys and girls, these came from experiences in their homes. Although the school did not explicitly engage in countering such gender stereotypes, engaging all students in all types of activities and encouraging all students in all kinds of subjects was helping to break these down.

The case study of the school makes it clear that it could be termed a learning organisation in the sense that it is continuously learning from others' experiences as well as from its own. For example, research studies on similar schools were carefully analysed for learning lessons, and the principal encouraged teachers to experiment and share their experiences. This is how the interactive whiteboard got introduced into one classroom and then from there to the entire school. It is also important that technology was not being viewed as a means in itself, but rather as a way of promoting interactive learning. Another example is that the principal and teachers showed a reflective attitude regarding their challenges, efforts, successes and failures. The development of an positive learning environment that took the students' social circumstances into account could largely be attributed to the direction provided by the principal, who was taking the lead in understanding the specific needs of the school, promoting team teaching and also allowing leadership skills to be developed in all teachers.

## II. Implementing a project, 'Change from Within', in a single-sex boys' secondary school, Jamaica

A former Vice Chancellor of the University of the West Indies (UWI), the late Sir Philip Sherlock, came across four inner-city schools in Jamaica that, independently of one another, were trying various ways of dealing with essentially the same problems of increasing violence and anti-social behaviour among boys. He brought them together under a programme called 'Change from Within', which involved a team of scholars at UWI in an applied research project to find ways of building the self-esteem of students, which in his opinion lay at the root of the problems. The principals, a few support staff and a the research team met as a Circle of Friends once a month to share experiences and ideas, plan strategies for action and learn how to improve leadership skills. A range of action research projects were undertaken, followed by strategic actions. This also promoted partnerships among all stakeholders including the community, teachers, parents and students. The programme expanded from four to seven schools during the period when it was being led by the University and later to 32 schools. The methodology developed on the basis of analysis of work being done in seven schools by the UWI team helped in the later expansion. Within a similar approach, each school had the freedom to adjust strategies according to its own specific situation. The focus was on:

i    creating a general awareness of the process;

ii   building social skills;

iii  establishing positive interdependence; and

iv   encouraging supportiveness and building a good
     interpersonal environment.

At another level, this also included elements of institution building within the schools. A number of workshops, training sessions and meetings were organised that provided guidance and assistance to teachers and encouraged them to identify the problems and generate workable solutions, map plans for action and implement strategies.

*...effective leadership required a set of important qualities. Some of these were: shared vision, commitment, team approach, problem solving/ conflict reduction skills, openness to learning and the ability to provide mutual support and to help manage the distress and challenges of change.*

The Circle of Friends meetings were central to the methodology and facilitated effective feedback and communicative planning. As group members were faced with the challenge of mobilising participants at a number of different levels, it became clear that effective leadership required a set of important qualities. Some of these were: shared vision, commitment, team approach, problem solving/ conflict reduction skills, openness to learning and the ability to provide mutual support and to help manage the distress and challenges of change. A series of school-based action research projects identified two factors as primarily responsible for the alienation of boys from schooling and education:

i    the nature of the early socialisation of boys by parents, their community
     and school; and

ii   the 'drill to kill' teaching and learning methods that were perceived as
     having increasingly marginalised boys and also girls from the schooling
     process.

The introduction of 'active learning' and innovative ways of engaging parents in the education of their children produced positive outcomes.

One of the schools implementing the CFW programme had once been a very prestigious school, educating Jamaica's elite. However, its image had changed as the school started taking children from poorer backgrounds and it faced problems of violence, gang-culture, drug addiction and under-performance. Poor family relations made the students undisciplined and insecure, and there was inter-school rivalry and conflict. On the teaching side, there was low teacher motivation, 'cliquism' among teachers and a lack of effective staff development programmes.

Three kinds of strategies were followed in an attempt to change boys' desires to conform to a stereotypical male identity and help them to develop a wider worldview. The first was to introduce strict rules relating to weapons and violence. It had been common for students to bring weapons to school and use them within and outside the school compound. A stringent ban was instituted on weapons and any instrument that could be used to inflict injury, as well as on cellular phone use, and metal detectors were introduced to catch violators of the rule. In addition, an emergency response team was formed to deal directly with violators. The second strategy was the introduction of effective and easily accessible counselling services to help boys shed the stereotypical masculine identity that stopped them from being emotional and inter-dependent. The death of some boys from the school was a great shock and led many boys to seek counselling, which helped them to accept different norms of living. Counselling has assisted students a great deal in facing and challenging peer pressure and forming a different kind of identity in due course. The third major strategy was to follow a transparent and inclusive approach where teachers, parents and the students themselves were treated with confidence and trust that helped the school win the support of all stakeholders.

Although there are still some problems of continued drug addiction among a small proportion of students, the school has succeeded to some extent in making the desired changes. It can perhaps change more if the curriculum and teaching practices also become more inclusive and empathetic.

## III. A basic education programme through distance mode, Lesotho

The Lesotho Distance Teaching Centre (LDTC), a department of the Ministry of Education and Training, was set up in 1972 to use distance education methods to address the needs of students who had not passed the final secondary education examinations. In 1977, a literacy and numeracy section, now the Centre for Basic Education, was added to provide literacy and skill training. This was started when it became clear that, despite the introduction of free primary education, some sections of society were not attending school. The reasons for this included the practice of having boys tend to livestock as well as the lack of value placed on education. The Learning Post (LP) programme was thus intended to cater for illiterate and semi-literate learners, a large proportion of whom are herdboys. It is very flexible and allows learners to complete the course at their own pace and time.

*The formal education system is not geared to deal with the specific needs of children coming from disadvantaged backgrounds, and learners who had dropped out stated that they had not felt comfortable there because of being older than other students and because of a lack of attention from teachers.*

Those enrolled in the LP programme gave as their motivation the hope of better employment opportunities and being able to deal with the exploitation that they often face. The formal education system is not geared to deal with the specific needs of children coming from disadvantaged backgrounds, and learners who had dropped out stated that they had not felt comfortable there because of being older than other students and because of a lack of attention from teachers. These drop outs largely came from uneducated and poor households, where almost all mothers were housewives and fathers were farmers. The flexibility helped them cope with their need to also help support their families and engage in practices such as cattle grazing. Although not equivalent to primary education, the programme covers basic literacy and numeracy skills in addition to some vocational skills. All the respondents who were consulted stated that the programme has had a positive impact on the learners and their communities. Graduates of the programme have been actively participating in community-based development projects, which was seen as a good use of the skills acquired through the programme. There have been more male students – a large number of them herdboys – in the LP programme than females students.

However, although the programme has had a positive impact and helped a number of children and adolescents acquire skills that they would not have acquired otherwise, it has been questioned on several grounds. The LP programme does not provide learners with a full cycle of primary or basic education and hence it cannot be considered as equivalent to the primary stage. It thus does not appear to be in conformity with the rights approach as it provides an inferior substitute for poor children, a criticism often made of alternatives that do not have the same or equivalent curricula. In addition, the relevance of the present curriculum has been questioned and the need has been highlighted to include additional topics such as conflict resolution, HIV/AIDS, career guidance, etc. A number of respondents suggested that the nature and quality of vocational skills need to change if the learners are expected to use these to find employment.

The low monthly honoraria paid to the programme administrators and teachers has led to most of the staff being middle-aged women as well as to a high incidence of turnover. Despite this, however, the level of motivation among these administrators/ teachers is usually observed to be high, one of the major reasons for the quality of delivery remaining acceptable despite adverse conditions. At the same time, it became clear in the process of consultation that motivation alone cannot sustain the programme and a number of interventions are required to improve it further. Major obstacles to improvement include the lack of a conducive environment and of adequate facilities for schooling. The respondents, particularly the administrators, indicated that the schools' proprietors do not allow the programme administrators to use their facilities. This confirms the finding of almost all evaluations undertaken for LDTC, which have recommended the more active involvement of stakeholders such as school proprietors, field-based education officers and parents/ guardians to improve the environment.

The LP programme relies heavily on the print and face-to-face modes of delivery, and there appeared to be widespread agreement that the use of modern technology would make the programme more accessible and cost-effective. This is especially relevant given the mountainous and remote nature of the terrain. However, while reception of Radio Lesotho is generally good throughout the country, its increased use as an education tool would only be possible if poor communities could be provided with radios.

For a number of reasons, the retention rates are apparently not very high in the LP programme. The most important has to do with the herdboys' lifestyle, as those who are employed tend to change employers and so may move from the district or locality in which they were able to participate in the programme. Even when the boys herd their own cattle, the long working day makes it difficult for them to attend classes in the evening. Attendance may also be sporadic as boys tend to spend longer periods at the cattle post during winter while girls are retained at home for help during harvesting periods. It is obvious that the whole issue of child labour needs to be addressed as these practices clash with any form of schooling. Sometimes herdboys join circumcision school, after which they discontinue other forms of education. Early marriages are common, and girls are often not permitted to go back to class after marriage or pregnancy. Language also acts as a barrier in some cases due to not everyone speaking Sesotho (the main language).

## IV. A vocational education alternative to secondary education, Samoa

Don Bosco Technical Centre is a single-sex boys' institution that responds to the needs of marginalised boys who have dropped out of regular formal secondary schools. It aims to facilitate their holistic development through an emphasis on technology education, career preparation and opportunities to develop social awareness. The Centre opened in 1989 with 32 students and had 250 in 2005. Most of the students come from the rural villages of the two largest islands: Upolu and Savaii.

*The boys in the Centre revealed that teaching and teacher-related factors had been the most important barriers to their achievement in regular mainstream schools.*

The four-year programme of study at the Centre focuses on design and technology associated with woodwork, metalwork, plumbing, mechanical engineering and boat building and includes theory, practical applications and information about the range of available career possibilities. Students are also offered courses in mathematics, communication skills, basic literacy, Samoan culture and religion. In addition, the Centre seeks to develop in its students the virtues of honesty, integrity, responsibility, trust and loyalty and strives to foster a commitment towards religious and moral convictions. It operates a flexible arrangement whereby students may leave on finding employment. Students who remain at the Centre for the duration of four years have a very high rate of success in terms of finding a job or continuing on to further studies.

The boys in the Centre revealed that teaching and teacher-related factors had been the most important barriers to their achievement in regular mainstream schools. They cited corporal punishment, threatening language, favouritism and lack of attention to weak students as examples of teachers' negative attitude towards boys from poorer families. The curriculum and pedagogy were described as narrow and uninspiring, with teachers failing to provide feedback and differential learning for varying abilities. There were also home-related factors that had caused them to drop out, the most common of which was the inability to pay school fees and meet other school costs. Girl-related factors included the fact that boys perceived girls to be distracting and feared being ridiculed in front of them due to lack of relationship skills. It appears that poor performance was also due to poor knowledge of the English language, which is the medium of instruction in secondary schools. A test of students entering the Centre showed that none of them had the proficiency required for learning other subjects through that language.

Most of the students at the Centre are there to obtain the skills necessary to finding a way to earn a living in order to pay back a perceived debt to parents, church and society. Students reported a great sense of achievement at the Centre in terms of learning skills related to technology and its application, development of appropriate attitudes, values and behaviour, and other life skills. They spoke of developing a sense of purposefulness, a keenness to learn and a disciplined lifestyle. Many of them reported improvement in language skills, and they also made special mention of communication skills, including increased confidence to interact with audiences of different sizes and ages. In addition, the boys appreciated the feelings of independence and self-confidence that came from being allowed to design and complete projects on their own. They felt respected and cared for.

The students identified seven principles that had led to their high level of support for the Centre and for their good performance: (1) enabling school environment, (2) school leadership, attitudes and philosophy, (3) nature of the curriculum, (4) education for life, (5) teachers' attitudes and philosophy, (6) teachers' pedagogical knowledge and skills and (7) teacher-student relationship.

The school stresses the importance of respectful and meaningful dialogue between teachers and students, principal and students, and students and students. Ways in which this is created include an annual residential one-week retreat for the entire school and regular whole school meetings with the principal. Students agreed that these meetings, which are used to challenge, motivate and counsel, had a great impact on them. A collective identity and cooperative attitude is also developed through the Centre's participation in outside-school events – including competing in the long boat (*fautasi*) races and sporting competitions and performing traditional dances. Students' achievements are highlighted in order to increase their self-esteem and self-image. Corporal punishment is not allowed.

The combination of theory with practical and workplace experience is clearly considered an effective approach by both students and teachers. An emphasis on interpersonal skills, understanding gender-related issues, diversity, decision-making skills, creative thinking and problem-solving skills, analytical skills for assessing self and others, information-gathering skills, coping and stress-management skills prepare them for life. The teacher-student relationship appeared to be relaxed and based on trust and respect, with teachers showing confidence in students' ability to do things on their own and students appreciating the special attention given to those who were perceived to be weak.

*The combination of theory with practical and workplace experience is clearly considered an effective approach by both students and teachers.*

There is no doubt that the Centre has helped these boys develop worthwhile skills and values including knowledge of various technologies, positive attitudes and behaviours, life and workplace skills, and spirituality. A language test also indicated an improvement in language and literacy as a result of their time at Don Bosco. On the other hand, the school also seems to reinforce the students' traditional notions of masculinity. Although this has helped in giving the students an identity and a purpose, it fails to change gender relations in the long run and therefore needs to be questioned.

Considering the fact that not much is known about the construction of masculinity in Samoan society and how, if at all, that interacts with school processes to contribute to boys' underachievement, it is difficult to arrive at definitive conclusions. The philosophies about maleness, masculinity and boys' ability to process themselves as males in Samoa and the interactions between these philosophies, practices and some of the evident patterns for males such as suicide and underachievement need to be studied further. With such deep-rooted beliefs in the role of the male in serving the family, it would be important to find out what happens to males' notions of dignity when they find themselves in positions of underachievement at school and then in the community if they are unable to get paid employment.

# HOW TO ADDRESS THE ISSUE: LESSONS AND QUESTIONS FROM THE INITIATIVES

The case studies of these four initiatives, one each of a formal school from mainstream systems in Australia and Jamaica, and two of outside-formal system, one using a distance mode for primary education in Lesotho and the other a means for alternative secondary education in Samoa, provide certain interesting insights regarding ways to address the issue of boys' underachievement. There are obvious limitations to generalising from case studies, and it is important to be aware of those caveats before applying the lessons on a wider scale. Nevertheless, the case studies succeed in providing valuable pointers for policy and programmatic solutions, and also raise questions for further research that would help in understanding the phenomenon better.

## School leadership plays a major role

Boys' underachievement, either in terms of participation or performance, is a result of a complex interplay of forces; it is not a creation of school processes alone. As such, it would be unfair to expect schools to provide a complete solution. Nonetheless, the case studies from Australia, Jamaica and Samoa clearly reveal that schools can make a difference. The three schools were dealing with difficult circumstances in different contexts – an Australian school facing children coming from diverse ethnic and low socio-economic backgrounds, Jamaican students practicing violence and Samoan students having failed in the mainstream schooling system – and used reformed management and pedagogical practices to succeed in helping students achieve.

In all three cases, school leadership played a very important role. The principals of the three schools have been a source of inspiration to their teachers as well as students. They have taken bold decisions regarding introducing reforms in management as well as teaching practices, and carried them through. They have shown signs of leading a learning organisation in continuously seeking new opportunities to learn and promote experimentation by colleagues. The environment in these schools helped develop leadership skills among teachers in general, reflecting the principals' leadership and managerial skills.

## An emphasis on cooperation, confidence-building and conflict resolution helps create an enabling environment

An emphasis on cooperation, confidence building and conflict resolution as against competition and rivalries appears to help in creating an enabling school environment for teachers as well as students. The focus on cooperation even in classroom organisation in the Australian school succeeded in creating an ethos where teachers are dependent on each other and young primary grade children also identify mutual dependence and teamwork as essential skills. The 'Change from Within' project in Jamaica focused on cooperation, and the participating principals not only learnt from one another but also passed on the principles of shared vision and teamwork to their teachers and indirectly to students. Students in the Samoan school clearly identified the creation of space for continuous dialogue between teachers and students as an important positive feature of the school. These practices helped create an environment of trust. This proved to be critical in developing a sense of self-worth among boys, a key requirement for better performance and achievement at any age.

*An emphasis on cooperation, confidence building and conflict resolution as against competition and rivalries appears to help in creating an enabling school environment for teachers as well as students.*

## A focus on active learning and respect for students helps to engage them

The focus on active teaching-learning processes, as against practices that require children to sit passively and learn, helped in engaging students and improving their achievement levels. These practices have to be chosen on the basis of age-appropriateness. The primary school-age boys and girls in the Australian school enjoyed working on the electronic board that allowed them space for experimentation and discovery, whereas the secondary school-age boys in the Samoan school appreciated undertaking projects from the beginning to the end on their own, and both sets of children identified these activities as confidence-boosting and leading to better learning. The experience of the Australian school showed that both sexes enjoyed active and participatory learning as compared to those practices that did not require them to engage themselves. The case studies do not provide space for this analysis for secondary-stage students as both the schools under consideration (Jamaica and Samoa) are single-sex boys' schools.

Respect for students, irrespective of their age, emerges as an important factor that helps them develop respect for teachers and appreciation of teachers' efforts. Boys in the Jamaican school and Samoan centre clearly felt respected, which made them take their teachers more seriously. In this context, it is interesting to see that the principles that are emerging as successful in contributing to better performance of boys are also the ones that generally help any student, boy or girl, to perform better.

## Female teachers a barrier: myth or reality?

*...it is interesting to see that the principles that are emerging for being successful in contributing to better performance of boys are also the ones that generally help any student, boy or girl, to perform better.*

A preponderance of female teachers in schools in certain countries, especially in the Caribbean and Pacific in addition to the developed countries, is often cited as a characteristic of school that deprives boys of suitable role models. The initiatives studied here do not provide any definitive indicators in this regard. The Australian school is co-educational, with the majority of teachers being women. This did not seem to be creating any problems for the boys. However, this is a primary school and it could be argued that the sex of the teacher does not matter so much at that age. The majority of teachers in the Lesotho distance learning centres are also women. Although this is a primary education programme, a number of students belong to the secondary age-group, and they have not provided any negative feedback about teachers. On the contrary, teachers' motivation and role were cited as major reasons for the success (albeit limited) of a programme that operated under adverse situations. The remaining two schools are single-sex boys' schools for secondary-age students with all male teachers. Students are comfortable with teachers but it is not clear how they would have responded to women teachers under similar management or teaching practices. These case studies do not provide any negative experience of students in other schools. It is, therefore, difficult to arrive at a definite conclusion in this regard. Limited evidence from the case studies suggest that it is not the presence or absence of female teachers but the adoption of a particular kind of management and teaching practices that make a real difference.

In this context, it would also be important in any future research to raise the issue of the kind and type of various male role models that are available in society and school, and their impact on the construction of masculine identity.

## Are single-sex schools a solution?

Single-sex schools for boys are another solution often offered to tackle boys' underachievement. It is difficult to arrive at a definite solution on the basis of the case studies in this regard as well. The Australian co-educational school does not face any problem and nor does Lesotho's distance teaching programme. It is not very clear to what extent the single-sex situations in the Jamaican school and the Samoan centre have benefited students. Therefore, it cannot be said with any degree of confidence that the change that was achieved in these schools could not have been achieved in a co-educational situation with similar school management and pedagogical practices. The Jamaican experience suggests that simply being a single-sex school at the outset did not automatically make the boys less alienated and better performers. It requires greater enquiry to arrive at any definitive inference in this regard.

## Alternative modes of schooling have potential

The Lesotho Distance Teaching Centre (LDTC) in Southern Africa and the Don Bosco Technical Centre in Samoa are the two examples of outside-mainstream systems of schooling identified in this study. Lesotho's Centre strives to provide a basic education to herdboys whose duties often prevent them from attending formal schooling. Since the under-participation of boys in Lesotho is primarily due to socio-economic and cultural reasons, the distance mode is seen as a solution. However, the courses currently offered by the LDTC are not equivalent in terms of curriculum and quality to formal schooling and hence do not showcase the potential of open and distance learning (ODL) as a complementary system for marginalised groups to obtain access to education for all.

During the LDTC's early days, in the mid-1970s, its work on literacy and numeracy for herdboys was considered exemplary. The Centre had developed workbooks and games that could be used in groups with the help of a trained leader. The project took several years to develop and eventually received the recognition of an international award. While the LDTC still survives, its current results are mixed. The print-based correspondence courses that are currently used to support the herdboys have done little to improve access to education in the country (nor do these course incorporate the principles that underpin the methodology of ODL, which includes structure and support from a provider)[7]; the institution as a whole lacks resources and is therefore unable to develop; and morale is low among LDTC staff. Further, the innovative vision of linking in-school and out-of-school education has not been realised (Jenkins, 1993).

*There are...examples in sub-Saharan Africa where ODL, used as a pedagogical alternative, has been successful in providing basic and secondary level education to out-of-school children and youth.*

There are, however, examples in sub-Saharan Africa where ODL, used as a pedagogical alternative, has been successful in providing basic and secondary level education to out-of-school children and youth. These include the Botswana Centre for Distance and Open Learning (BOCODOL), the Namibian College of Open Learning (NAMCOL), the Nigerian National Commission for Nomadic Education (NCNE) and the Interactive Radio Instruction (IRI) initiative in Zambia. Both the Nigerian and Zambian initiatives provide primary education to children with the aim of improving literacy. NCNE provides primary education to children of nomadic pastoralists and migrant fishing communities via suitable delivery mechanisms such as boat schools and other mobile schools. The Zambian initiative broadcasts lessons over the radio to learners in IRI centres using an interactive approach. Children (from 8 to 10 years) are organised into listening groups that meet at the centres under the guidance of mentors, who themselves are school leavers (and who have subsequently been trained by qualified staff from the Zambian Ministry of Education).

At the secondary level, BOCODOL in Botswana and NAMCOL in Namibia are two parastatal or semi-autonomous national institutions offering programmes for out-of-school adolescents and adults who are unable to continue their secondary level studies in formal schools for various reasons. Both institutions offer courses leading to the Junior Secondary Certificate (Grade 10) and the General Certificate of Secondary Education (Grade 12) and employ a combination of face-to-face and specially designed ODL print materials

---

7    Adapted from the definition provided on The Open and Distance Learning Quality Council website: *www.odlqc.org.uk/g-odl.htm*; see also *www.col.org/colweb/site/pid/2904*.

supported by radio, audiotapes and, most recently, computers. In addition to these secondary level programmes, both institutions are expanding their repertoire by providing vocational and other pre-tertiary courses. The majority of learners enrolled in NAMCOL live in rural areas of northern Namibia or in severely disadvantaged urban areas. BOCODOL offers programmes throughout the country, including special programmes for nomads through which students have an opportunity to access a series of community learning centres as they move across the northern part of the country (Dodds, 2003; Green and Trevor-Deutsch, 2002; Mukhopadhyay and Phillips, 1994).[8]

Don Bosco Technical Centre's emphasis on high-quality vocational education at secondary level is well placed as a choice for post-basic education. However, such a choice cannot be promoted exclusively for boys and that too only for those who have failed in the mainstream system of schooling. This would undermine the importance of vocational education for anyone, including those who perform well in the regular secondary system, and also undermine the importance of reforming the mainstream system in a manner that allows students of both sexes from all kinds of backgrounds to learn and progress.

## Schools should actively question stereotyped gender identity

*...management and pedagogical practices that promote cooperation and active participation can help somewhat in breaking down traditional gender divides.*

None of the four case-study schools/ centres, except the one in Jamaica to some extent, deliberately sought to address the issue of questioning prevalent or stereotyped gender identity and constructing a new gender identity that would help boys deal more effectively with schooling processes. However, the Australian school inadvertently succeeded in achieving this objective by adopting certain practices due to the leadership style of the principal and the kind of pedagogical practices that the school was adopting. This shows that management and pedagogical practices that promote cooperation and active participation can also help somewhat in breaking down traditional gender divides. Nonetheless, evidence from the same school also shows that more deliberate and active engagement is required in this respect as children from a very early age start forming and responding to social gender identities that they get exposed to in and outside the school, with home and family playing a major role.

---

8    For other examples of open schooling, see the National Institute of Open Schooling (NIOS), India: *www.nos.org/*; Open School BC (Canada): *www.openschool.bc.ca/index.html*; the Alberta Distance Learning Centre (Canada): *www.adlc.ca/home/*; and The Correspondence School of New Zealand: *www.correspondence.school.nz/*.

The Samoan case study suggests that the Centre tried to uphold and reinforce the 'traditional' masculine identity of boys, emphasising their role of protector, and it helped them in developing a positive self-image and identity. However, it does not provide a solution for all schools, especially in the mainstream system, if the vision is to develop a society where sex is not used for any form of discrimination and gender relations are based on equality of treatment and opportunity. The Jamaican school provides more interesting insights as it succeeded in breaking the pressure of peer-endorsed masculine behaviour that leads to violence and other negative behaviour and is a major reason for boys' underperformance. As in the case of the Australian school, the adoption of particular kinds of management and pedagogical practices that emphasise cooperation and trust-building has helped. This confirms that such practices have great potential for addressing issues related to masculine gender identity. In addition, certain specific strategies such as counselling played a major role in breaking the myth that boys should not show the need for emotional support and care.

> *... it is important for schools to play an active role in questioning the prevalent gender identities to address the issue of boys' underachievement. The experiences show that it is also possible to do so.*

It emerges that it is important for schools to play an active role in questioning the prevalent gender identities to address the issue of boys' underachievement. The experiences show that it is also possible to do so. However, an in-depth analysis of curricular design and classroom practices in diverse situations can provide greater insights and more pointed indicators.

# THE NEED FOR FURTHER RESEARCH AND ITS NATURE

This report has outlined the issue of boys' underachievement in the Commonwealth, discussing some of the possible causes and analysing some of the initiatives that appear to have addressed the issue. In this process it has also provided a few broad policy and programmatic suggestions. However, clearly there remains a lot more to be researched for greater understanding and more pointed policy recommendations. This includes:

1 In-depth and qualitative gender analysis of management and pedagogical practices in secondary schools operating under diverse situations and contexts: co-education, single-sex for boys, single-sex for girls, female-majority teachers, mixed-sex teachers and male-majority teachers. This could be undertaken in several countries following the same research design but with an understanding of the social and economic background in which the school operates and the nature of the boys' underachievement prevalent in that particular country or region.

2 A study of teenaged boys in diverse situations and contexts to understand the construction of masculinities and its impact on educational choices and processes.

3 A study of the relationship between boys' underachievement and gender privilege in diverse situations and contexts through analysis of statistics from different countries using both education (participation as well as performance data) and socio-economic and political indicators.

4 Identification of best practices, including the application of open, distance and technology-mediated learning and associated challenges and potentials.

# CONCLUSION

It is evident from the above analyses that boys' under-participation and underperformance both have their roots in a few general issues and characteristics of societies as well as education systems. There is also a lot of similarity in the manner in which this combination operates against boys' schooling participation in some countries as it works against girls' participation in many others. A combination of paucity of school spaces and societal demands regarding occupational or gender roles leads to under-participation of boys in countries such as Lesotho and Samoa whereas similar lack of adequate schooling facilities coupled with strict demands of gender roles work against girls' schooling in many Sub-Saharan African and South and West Asian countries. The solution, as is well known, lies in not only expanding the school spaces and facilities but also challenging established notions of gender roles, relations and stereotypes using all possible interventions inside and outside the school.

Transforming gender roles and relations in order to relieve the huge pressure of conforming to established notions of 'masculinities' is critical in addressing the issue of boys' underperformance, which especially occurs in countries or sub-national areas that have succeeded in expanding access and girls participate in schooling in high numbers. Increased participation of girls in situations where education was not their traditional domain signifies a shift in gender relations. Men start viewing this as shrinking the space for themselves and look for domains that are exclusively for men and therefore 'masculine'. Education itself, including good performance, is labelled as feminine, and not working hard and doing well is considered to be 'cool' by boys.

The case studies showed that schools can make a difference provided they focus on certain processes that promote cooperation and respect and question gender stereotypes. It is also interesting to note that most of these processes are such that they help both boys and girls and raise the quality of schooling in general. The case studies also suggest that changes in schools' curricula and processes are more crucial than having male teachers or all-male classrooms. Therefore, while there is a need for more researchers to develop a more nuanced understanding, there is also a need for this realisation that the issue of boys' underachievement is not de-linked from the issue of female social positioning, and school reforms based on the principle of gender equality can go a long way in addressing the root of the problem.

# PART II:
# the case studies

# 4.
# Australia: socialisation and socio-economics

There is almost no gender disparity at primary school level in Australia. The net enrolment ratio (NER) in 2002-2003 was 94.3 per cent for boys and 95.1 per cent for girls, leading to a gender parity index (GPI) of 1.01. The disparity increases at secondary stage but still remains insignificant. In 2002-2003, the NER for boys at secondary stage was 87.0 per cent whereas it was 89.1 per cent for girls, with a GPI of 1.02.[9] Therefore, although the lower likelihood of boys compared to girls completing their secondary education and entering tertiary education has been a subject of discussion in Australia, the issue of boys' underachievement in the country mainly relates to under-performance.

A number of performance indicators for secondary stage education in the 1990s indicated underachievement of boys in different parts of the country. For example:

- aggregate results at Year 12 level show that in the 1999 New South Wales Higher School Certificate, for subjects studied by more than 100 students, girls' average marks were up to 11 per cent higher than boys' in 36 of the 40 subjects;

- in Queensland in 1998, a greater proportion of girls were in the top performance bands in 36 of 45 Year 12 subjects;

- in South Australia in 1998, a higher proportion of girls were in the top performance bands in 27 of 34 Year 12 subjects;

9    These data are sourced from UNESCO, 2006. Gender parity index refers to girls' NER/ boys' NER.

- the difference between boys' and girls' average results in the New South Wales Tertiary Entrance Score (TES) widened from 0.6 marks in 1981 to 19.4 marks in 1996, with the difference increasingly rapidly in the early 1990s.

As a result, the relative achievement of boys and girls in Year 12 assessments has featured prominently in popular as well as academic debate.

# WHAT DOES PISA INDICATE?

Australia has been part of the international tests known as the Programme for International Student Assessment (PISA), which have been conducted on a large sample in Organisation for Economic Cooperation and Development (OECD) countries and a few developing countries every three years since 2000. The available analysis of PISA results for Australia helps in getting a more nuanced understanding of the issue.[10] PISA 2000 focused on assessing students' capacity to apply knowledge and skills to reading, mathematics and science. PISA 2003 focused more on mathematics and PISA 2006 on science. The assessment includes a variety of tests to examine different kinds of skills and knowledge of 15-year-olds. PISA results for 2000 show that Australia was one of the top scorers in all three areas – reading, mathematics and scientific literacy – and was also well above the OECD average in all of them.

PISA 2000 showed that there was no significant difference in girls' and boys' performance in mathematics and science in any of the Australian states or territories. PISA 2003 also did not show any gender difference in overall mathematical literacy in Australia. However, almost twice as many males as females achieved the highest PISA proficiency level in mathematics, indicating no evidence of boys' underachievement in this subject. The situation changes, however, when it comes to reading literacy. Girls performed better than boys, though the level of difference was lower in Australia than most other OECD countries. The level of the gap also varied between different states and territories, being significantly higher in some as compared to others.

There is a correlation between achievement scores and socio-economic status in most countries, with those from poorer socio-economic backgrounds performing worse than their counterparts from more prosperous backgrounds.

---

10   The analysis of PISA results is based on (i) files downloaded on PISA 2003 from the Australian Council for Educational Research (ACER) site, (ii) ACER and OECD, 2001 and (iii) Australian Bureau of Statistics, 2005 (all downloads from the Internet).

Australia is no exception to this. In addition, the Australian analysis also shows that socio-economic status compounds the difference between boys and girls in terms of their reading literacy, with boys from low socio-economic backgrounds found to be almost twice as likely to be in the lowest quarter of reading literacy results than girls from similar backgrounds. The results for mathematics and science also show a relationship between socio-economic status and the likelihood of achieving a low score, but this is the same for both boys and girls in science and not large enough to be significant in mathematics. This suggests that schools may play a larger role in the development of mathematical and scientific skills than they do in reading skills, a conclusion corroborated by the fact that students in Australia who came from a non-English speaking home background performed at an equivalent level in mathematical literacy to students whose home language was English, but at a lower level in reading and scientific literacy. Students' results also showed some differences according to the location of their schools. Students in provincial cities performed as well as students in large cities and major urban areas, but students whose schools were in remote areas performed less well than other students in reading and scientific literacy. There was no difference in mathematical literacy results by location of school. The environment outside school appears to play an important role in building reading literacy and, to some extent, scientific literacy.

*There is a correlation between achievement scores and socio-economic status in most countries, with those from poorer socio-economic backgrounds performing worse than their counterparts from more prosperous backgrounds.*

An analysis of results related to 'engagement with reading' provides some insights into the reading literacy scores. 'Engagement with reading' reflects how much students like reading, how much they enjoy talking about books and go to libraries, whether reading is a favourite hobby, and so on. Australian students were at the same level as the OECD average in this area with – as in most countries – girls scoring significantly higher than boys. Attitudes towards reading were moderately strongly related to reading achievement in Australia, where a third of the students said they never read for enjoyment. While this percentage was higher in a few other countries, the achievement difference in reading literacy between students who never read for enjoyment and those who read for an hour or two each day was greater in Australia than in any other country.

It is also noteworthy that though nearly 40 per cent of Indigenous students in Australia performed at par with average, in general they performed at a lower level than the non-Indigenous students in the three assessment areas: reading literacy, mathematical literacy and scientific literacy, with results below the OECD mean. Gender differences were similar to the other Australian students, with females outperforming the males in reading literacy. No significant gender differences were found in mathematical or scientific literacy. The influence of home background factors on performance was examined. The mean socio-economic status of Indigenous students was lower than that of non-Indigenous students, and resources such as books were fewer in their homes. There was, however, a higher level of equity, with less difference in performance between low and high socio-economic status Indigenous students than for the performance between low and high socio-economic status non-Indigenous students.[11]

What is significant is that the most important school factor related to achievement in Australia, as in most other countries, was the overall socio-economic background of the student body. Other factors such as instructional climate and practices at the schools were also related to achievement. For example, Australia scored relatively high, together with the United Kingdom, on the index of teacher support, as perceived by students. Performance is positively correlated with greater opportunities to ask questions and Australia also ranked quite high on this indicator.

*An examination of several facts reveals that the difference in socialisation that boys and girls experience might be playing an important role in enabling girls to perform better in reading literacy and language.*

The analysis of PISA results makes it clear that gender is only one dimension of differentiation that characterises performance outcomes of 15-year-olds in Australia. Socio-economic status turns out to be more critical for both boys and girls. However, what makes gender important is that similar trends of no significant difference in mathematics and science scores and a significant difference in favour of girls in reading literacy are observed for all socio-economic and social groups. An examination of several facts reveals that the difference in socialisation that boys and girls experience might be playing an important role in enabling girls to perform better in reading literacy and language. The fact that boys have much less 'engagement with reading' reflects their socialisation pattern where from an early age they are encouraged to take part in outdoor

---

11   The details provided here on Indigenous students have been taken from De Bortoli and Cresswell, 2004 (downloaded from *www.acer.edu.au/research/special_topics/ind_edu/ research.html*).

and physical activities, whereas girls are encouraged to enjoy indoor activities. The experiences of boys and girls in terms of the kinds of play materials they possess, the sports they are encouraged to participate in, the activities they are engaged in by parents and others are usually quite different from one another. The nature of activities that are considered suitable for girls is usually such that it helps in building better language and interactive skills, including an inclination towards reading, whereas the opposite is true for boys. This explains boys' relatively lower performance in reading literacy to some extent.

In this context, it also becomes important to understand the role of socialisation in relation to mathematics and science achievement scores. Mathematics and science have traditionally been perceived as 'masculine' subjects almost everywhere in the world. A focus on girls' education and women's rights emanating from various movements changed this to some extent so that doing well in what had traditionally been considered a male domain became a matter of pride for girls. Unlike language, school interventions play a major role in subjects such as mathematics and science, and hence in countries where girls attend schools regularly, they have also started performing well in these subjects. However, the fact that girls feel less confident in their abilities despite performing as well as boys in mathematics[12] is a reflection of the stereotypes that continue to exist in society. This is also confirmed by recent research on school subject selection and subsequent study and work participation in Australia, which found that males are still much more likely than females to be taking advanced mathematics and science at senior secondary school and to move into mathematics and science-related courses in higher education.[13]

The above analysis indicates that factors similar to those that kept girls away from selecting subjects such as mathematics and science are contributing in boys' underachievement in language in Australia, at least to some extent. Socialisation and gender stereotypes in different walks of life get reflected in subject selections and performance outcomes. Schools can play a role in changing this, but it is not clear to what extent they can make a difference. The following case study of a school located in the outskirts of a capital city in Australia provides some insights into several of these issues.

---

12   As reported by UNESCO, 2006.
13   As reported in Thomson et al, 2004.

# A GOVERNMENT PRIMARY SCHOOL IN QUEENSLAND

## Background

An inner-city government co-educational primary school located in a multicultural setting in Queensland was identified for the purpose of the case study. The school was chosen because of its leadership, its attempts to implement whole-school pedagogical reform and the impact of these factors on the educational engagement and participation of all students including boys. The school was studied in-depth by Lingard et al (2002), who had identified it as "one of the best schools for boys". The school was involved in the Productive Pedagogy trial programme and had noted no difference in literacy scores between boys and girls, which was attributed to the learning culture within the school. In addition the school has recorded high literacy scores on national and state tests for both boys and girls. It has embraced multi-age classes and co-operative learning, and has a strong focus on professional development for teachers and on collaborative decision-making. This school was identified for a re-visit to try and reassess its practices and extract lessons.

Located in a low-income area and opened in 1978, the school has over 800 students and 65 teachers (the majority women). It has faced multiple challenges mainly because of the socio-economic and linguistic background of the students that it receives. Most of the children come from poor families, often struggling with livelihood choices. The incidence of dependence on welfare schemes for survival is high and so is the rate of crime. Many households have been living on the dole (state-subsidised benefits) for two to three generations. A number of parents reportedly have criminal backgrounds and have spent time in jail. The tradition of education is not very strong in these households. These factors get reflected in a variety of ways. As revealed by the principal and the teachers, there is some level of student absenteeism and late arrival to school is also not uncommon. The difficult home situations deprive children of a conducive environment for studying. A number of teachers raised the issue of needing to concentrate on behaviour management and the impact this has on learning.

The school has an Indigenous student population of approximately 5 per cent as well as a high proportion of students of Asian and Pacific Island descent.

The principal estimated that around 10 per cent of the students have language difficulties at school due to English being their second language. In the six observed classrooms were students from Cambodia, the Cook Islands, Fiji, New Zealand, the Philippines, Russia, Serbia, Samoa and the Ukraine, as well as Indigenous Australians, Torres Strait Islanders and Anglo Australians. Classrooms with students having a variety of mother tongues pose a serious challenge to teachers. In addition, the school also gets a high number of students with special learning needs despite the fact that other schools in the area have specialised in this field. There is a Special Needs Unit in the school with seven staff members and around 70 students. The principal feels that recognised special needs are only one aspect of the problem, however, with over a quarter of the students being in need of some kind of support.

The case of this school is especially relevant considering that

i    socio-economic status is the most important factor related to underperformance of students in Australia;

ii   boys' relative underperformance is evidenced largely in reading literacy; and

iii  the difference between boys' and girls' achievement outcomes for reading literacy is wider for lower socio-economic status groups.

The school has been maintaining a database of progress of students, and this shows a positive change over the years. The earlier study by Lingard et al (2002) had noted a student-friendly school culture, with no evidence of poor behaviour, and where students were provided with the social skills to avoid conflicts. Absenteeism was not a problem except in certain specific cases in the year that research was conducted, and the school had had no suspensions or exclusions and had only one bullying incident noted in the Annual Report. This progress is attributed to the pedagogical reform adopted by the school. The school claims that this has helped all students, those who had traditionally been underachievers and those who had been performing well. Although it would require more research to prove that the school has made a difference in terms of impact on students' performance, especially on boys' achievement, the general image as well as the experiences of students and teachers suggest that the school is 'different' and has been successful in creating an environment of optimism, hope and high expectations. The reasons for this success can be traced to imaginative and committed leadership from the principal and a number of reforms initiated in the school, including pedagogical practices as well as strategies for greater involvement of parents.

## What made learning experiences different

### An empathetic understanding of the socio-economic, linguistic and cultural background of students

The principal as well as most teachers who were interviewed showed an empathetic understanding of the socio-economic, linguistic and cultural background of students. This understanding was particularly evident in statements made by the principal. While he recognised the challenges posed by students' poor socio-economic status and multicultural background, he also saw this as an opportunity, as evidenced in his statement, "a lot of the multicultural dimensions in low socio-economic groups are advantageous". He emphasised the fact that though the students are currently facing poverty, many of these families come from very rich cultures that could be used positively. Most teachers also reflected a good understanding of backgrounds and the impact this could have on behaviour as well as learning. For instance, one teacher referred to the fact that many children suffer from malnutrition due to bad diets, which affected their attention span and motivation. Similar references were made regarding English not being the children's first language and their experiences of war and conflict in some cases. Overall, it appears that the school environment is such that teachers developed empathy for students' backgrounds and tried to face the challenge of resolving issues related to these. None of the students interviewed shared any negative experience from any teacher in this context.

> *Overall, it appears that the school environment is such that teachers developed empathy for students' backgrounds and tried to face the challenge of resolving issues related to these.*

Unlike many other schools facing similar problems, this school depicts a faith in children's inate desire and ability to learn, and the recognition of the fact that schools can actually play a negative role at times. The principal articulated this as:

> Kids basically want to learn. That is not their problem. That is a natural desire. They came well packaged with that right since birth …Schools can switch that off; individuals can switch that off.

### Teaching methods and learning opportunities: Focus on cooperation and engagement

The school focuses on cooperation and teamwork in its pedagogy and the kinds of learning opportunity it tries to create. It uses double teaching spaces, with two teachers working as a team to teach two grades. The physical arrangement of classes is such that the students' desks are placed at each end of the space in front of an ICT whiteboard and a blackboard, and a central area is used to do ground activities and to access the whiteboard.

The use of interactive ICT whiteboards is a special feature of the school, which has invested heavily in teaching aids. These boards use a data projector connected to a computer and give a large visual of the computer screen. Students and teachers are able to control the computer through the touch-sensitive whiteboard. Teachers create learning activities that are saved into a central directory accessible by other teachers. This, in effect, works as a digital library that gets expanded as teachers keep adding new activities. Although creating a new activity take a lot of time and energy, once this has been done, other teachers can easily use it. In the course of time, as new activities are added, the need to develop activities is expected to be substantially reduced.

Classroom observations showed that the use of ICT boards has tremendous potential for making learning interesting and engaging for children. Students enjoyed taking turns and discovering through the board new aspects of whatever they were learning. The board was used in a variety of ways. For example, it was used as a literacy aid where reading words were presented in the form of a PowerPoint presentation, and students in Grade 2 read the words out loud to much delight as these bounced around the page. In a science-based class where students were looking at the human body, the teachers accessed an interactive programme that allowed students to virtually dissect parts of the body and read about their properties. In a number of other classes, students were observed participating in activities to support mathematical skills such as addition, multiplication, division and subtraction. Teachers were united in their opinion regarding the success of these boards in keeping children engaged and more interested in learning, including children with special needs.

Students were also quite articulate when talking about the use of the technology in the classroom. They could identify elements such as not having to use an eraser, using hands to write and erase and not having to use a keyboard to control the computer, in addition to mentioning their enjoyment in playing games on the board. A number of these games had educational value (e.g., hangman, number-cruncher and snakes and ladders). Children also enjoyed other aspects of using the technology such as pulling up the keyboard, using the timer, writing text and converting it into a font, using symbols, colours and different fonts, customising text and images and so on. They also demonstrated writing math equations and converting them into a font.

Moreover, students who were interviewed cited skills such as teamwork and sharing as advantages of using the whiteboard. This indicates that the school has been successful in communicating these important messages to children. Given the fact that teaching social skills has been a central agenda of the school, this is definitely a marker of success. In general, there is a lot of focus on engaging children in a variety of activities in and outside the classroom, and both boys and girls appear to enjoy participating. Extra efforts are made to engage children needing special attention. For instance, the special education unit runs a full-fledged café once per week with the active involvement of students, giving them the opportunity to fully participate in a cooperative manner. No gender differentiation was observed in terms of work allocation and efforts to engage the children. The choice was guided by the level at which each child was in that particular subject.

> *...a generalised intervention can at times be unsuitable for specific children such as those from low socio-economic and varied cultural backgrounds.*

The school is also part of a larger project focusing on a new system of formative assessment where children and teachers both reflect on the progress made. The involvement of students in their own assessment ensures their engagement and ownership, leading to new kinds of learning. However, the principal also expressed his reservations about certain aspects of this project as some interventions can be far removed from the backgrounds of the kinds of students coming to the school. This concern also revealed the fact that a generalised intervention can at times be unsuitable for specific children such as those from low socio-economic and varied cultural backgrounds.

As observed by Lingard et al (2002), the school does not participate in inter-school competitive sport, and has explicitly rejected a 'deficit student' and 'deficit family' approach in interpreting students' learning and behaviours. They had noted that the curriculum focus was on environmental education and philosophy, and the children were taught how to resolve conflict by talking through issues. It did not have programmes in place specifically for boys. The researchers in that study had also noted the widespread engagement of students and reported that there were no observable gender differences. The emphasis on quality pedagogy and a supportive classroom and whole school environment, along with the teaching of skills to help students handle conflict and differences of opinion, appeared to be the factors contributing to the commendable outcomes (ibid).

The previous research (Lingard et al, 2002) also observed that while students were expected to treat teachers with respect, they were also able to engage in frank and open discussion, where disagreement was possible and where both teachers and students could express their opinions and usually reach a meaningful resolution. The intellectually challenging nature of classroom work, such as the introduction of philosophy into the classroom, within a supportive school environment, was identified as having great social as well as academic rewards.

### Confirming or breaking gender stereotypes?

While the teachers demonstrated awareness of the debate surrounding boys' underachievement, they struggled to find evidence of it at the school as in most cases it was female students who presented significant behavioural problems that had to be addressed with specific strategies beyond the classroom. When prompted, teachers talked about differences between boys and girls in terms of behaviour and learning, but no uniform pattern emerges from these statements. Depending on their individual experiences they came up with statements that often contradicted each other. If one teacher said "boys learn faster", another said, "boys just get really uninterested quite easily... they do lack motivation and they can be lazy", and yet another said "the boys do better...they just learn quicker than girls". Similarly, regarding girls, if one teacher said "some of them are a bit chatty...but they get their work done", another said, "my girls are well behaved, there's no problems there, they're just academically not at the level of the boys", and yet another said, "a lot of my girls are achieving, they're actually completing work of a higher quality than what the boys are". It is also important to point out that most teachers qualified their statements by adding that what they were saying did not apply to all. In general, what they were communicating through seemingly contradictory statements was that they had not really experienced major differences, a view actually expressed by some teachers.

Interviews with teachers, students and the principal as well as classroom observations suggested that the school did not have any specific intervention for boys or girls, and did not perceive gender to be a major issue per se. This was reflected in the fact that they did not articulate this as a challenge. However, the focus on actively engaging each child depending on her or his situation appeared to be taking care of children's needs adequately at the primary stage of education. This became apparent from some of the statements made by young students in their interviews.

A number of boys interviewed identified the arts as their favourite subject while mentioning that they also enjoyed doing mathematics on the whiteboard. This indicated that they did not see the subjects as 'feminine' or 'masculine'. This is important as art and reading are often labelled as 'feminine', making it difficult for boys to accept that they like these subjects, which then leads to poor performance. Also important is the fact that all of the stereotypical notions about boys and girls that children expressed in their interviews had emanated from their homes. For instance, one child responded to the issue of physical fights by saying that his mother and sisters always tell him that "boys are stronger". The implication was that if they are stronger they have to show that by fighting. Similarly, another boy said his mother takes him and not his sister everywhere she goes. These experiences are creating the notions of what is 'masculine' and what is 'feminine' and have started affecting their behaviour. The school experiences so far had not reinforced any of these ideas as the teachers could narrate examples of both boys and girls being punished and other such incidents.

Although the school did not explicitly engage in countering the gender stereotypes being created in the society, many of its interventions actually led to breaking stereotypes. This includes the engagement of all students in all types of activities and encouragement to all students for all kinds of subjects. In addition, one of the incidents narrated by students is worth noting. Two boys were discussing the 'lollypop lady' (a kind of volunteer who is traditionally a woman) when one of them said he could be one. The other pointed out that he would have to be a 'lollypop man' and that "dads never do it". The first one replied that this was not necessarily so, as the principal had performed this task once. The other one agreed. It is clear from the example that the principal's act had helped break the stereotype, and such interventions go a long way in creating alternative images.

### Community outreach

The school has been actively involved in trying to develop parenting skills and leadership among the community and engaging it in school activities. Although they feel that they have not been very successful, their ideas have been imaginative and their efforts have made some inroads. The need for a proactive approach in providing support to parents on parenting skills was strongly felt and some courses had been organised. Though this generated interest and parents enjoyed them, according to the principal, it did not lead to significant behaviour change. The school was planning a community renewal project focusing on the needs of young mothers on a range of issues including nutrition and nurturing through inter-agency personnel working on-site.

In order to build leadership among parents, the school has a system of having classroom parent representatives, with new people inducted every year. This has been running successfully and parents have responded well. The school also tried to involve parents as resource persons by giving them the opportunity to come and share with the children their experiences relating to their work. The response to this has not been overwhelming, but some parents responded and the intervention was successful to some extent.

## The School as a Learning Organisation

This case study makes it clear that this school could be termed a learning organisation in the sense that it is continuously learning from others' experiences as well from its own. A few examples of how the school has been learning and growing will help clarify this observation. In order to gain a better understanding of schools functioning in multicultural situations, the principal and teachers looked at a school where detailed research had been conducted on dealing with multicultural challenges. References were also made to other research and projects by the principal and teachers, reflecting their awareness of those interventions.

*This case study makes it clear that this school could be termed a learning organisation in the sense that it is continuously learning from others' experiences as well from its own.*

How the interactive ICT board got introduced into the classroom is also a revealing story. In 2003, the principal brought one such board to the school after he saw it being used in a school in England. This was placed in the staff room, but remained underused. A Grade 1 teacher, having seen the use of this board in some city school elsewhere, approached the principal to allow her to take this one to her classroom. She presented a detailed outline of how it would be used and was given permission to take it. She and another teacher, who were sharing the classroom in the cooperative system, experimented a lot and came up with many useful lessons and activities. On seeing and hearing this, other teachers also demonstrated interest. Two more teaching teams drew up proposals for the board's use in their classrooms and they too were provided with boards. Others followed suit and the school has now introduced this into every classroom. The fact that the principal encouraged teachers' initiatives and they learnt from each other shows an environment that is open and conducive to experimentation. The cooperative teaching practice also appears to have contributed to teachers developing a sense of shared responsibility. These are indicators of the school being a learning organisation.

It is also important that technology was not being viewed as an end in itself, but rather as a way of creating an interactive learning environment. The principal was emphatic in pointing out that this was all about pedagogy and a positive learning environment, and that the boards cannot be recommended to all schools in isolation of other aspects. The principal and teachers showed a reflective attitude regarding their challenges, efforts, successes and failures. They were honest in sharing their experiences. This too is a sign of a learning organisation. It was also clear that a lot of this could be attributed to the direction provided by the principal in allowing leadership skills to be developed in all teachers. The principal was taking the lead in understanding the specific needs of the school and promoting the whole school pedagogical reform that focused on team teaching and an interactive learning environment that takes the students' social circumstances into account.

*...a number of these interventions are designed in such a way that they help break down gender stereotypes and allow both boys and girls to realise their potential in learning. This definitely has lessons for other schools as well as for policy makers.*

Again, these observations are similar to those by Lingard et al (2002), who explained this school's success as a combination of intellectually demanding teaching and assessment, accompanied by a strong emphasis on supporting all students and recognising difference, the creation of a teacher professional learning community, and leadership practices that support the school culture. They thus concluded that "these appear to be the necessary ingredients for ensuring effective and engaging learning for students in schools across all locations" (ibid: 63).

## CONCLUSIONS

This school provides an example of how pedagogical reform practices can help in active engagement and higher learning levels of all children, boys and girls. The principal and teachers were unambiguous in communicating that they do not see boys' underachievement as a specific issue. They believe that an engaging learning process in an interactive and contextualised learning environment is the solution. The school faces serious challenges in terms of the socio-economic status and multicultural background of the children, but the combination of good leadership, pedagogical reform and efforts to understand the situation and involve the community has helped it achieve results. Although this is not their explicit aim, a number of these interventions are designed in such a way that they help break down gender stereotypes and allow both boys and girls to realise their potential in learning. This definitely has lessons for other schools as well as for policy makers. However, given the fact that children are exposed to a number of gender stereotypes in their home and the society in which they live, a conscious integration of some of the gender aspects in the process of pedagogical reform would perhaps ensure that the school is able to counter the societal influence.

# 5.
# Jamaica: alienation and high drop-out rates

Concern for boys' underachievement is quite high in several Commonwealth countries in the Caribbean region. As gender parity indices have improved for girls in recent years, educators and policy makers have started to focus attention on the relative underperformance of boys compared to girls, particularly at the secondary level and in their progression to post-secondary and tertiary education. At the same time, Jamaica is facing one of the highest homicides rates in the world, with most of the killings committed by young men. To deal with the problem of youth violence, education systems both in Jamaica and the region have to redefine their role in moulding socially and emotionally well-adjusted young people who are equipped with both a well-defined set of personal attributes and a predetermined range of aptitude and skills.

*Concern for boys' underachievement is quite high in several Commonwealth countries in the Caribbean region.*

## DEFINING THE PROBLEM

A survey of basic enrolment data in Jamaica shows that over a 13-year period boys have stayed fractionally behind girls in terms of primary and secondary participation when looking at net enrolment ratios (NER). However, the differences at primary level are quite marginal. A look at Table 7, for example, shows that primary NER for boys and girls went from level-pegging at 96 per cent in 1990/91 to a slight disparity of 94 per cent to 95 per cent respectively in 2002/2003, both registering a gender parity index (GPI) of an even 1.00.

## TABLE 7: ENROLMENT RATIOS IN PRIMARY EDUCATION, JAMAICA

| PRIMARY | | 1990/ 1991 | 1998/ 1999 | 2000/ 2001 | 2002/ 2003 | REGIONAL AVERAGE 2002/2003 |
|---|---|---|---|---|---|---|
| GROSS ENROLMENT RATIO (GER) (%) | MF | 101 | 95 | 100 | 100 | 119 |
| | M | 102 | 96 | 100 | 100 | 121 |
| | F | 101 | 95 | 99 | 99 | 118 |
| NET ENROLMENT RATIO (NER) (%) | MF | 96 | 90 | 95 | 95 | 96 |
| | M | 96 | 90 | 95 | 94 | 97 |
| | F | 96 | 90 | 95 | 95 | 96 |

Notes:   (a) Regional refers to the entire Caribbean
(b) Some data cover specific years or are an estimate. See the UNESCO Institute for Statistics (UIS) website for more information (www.uis.unesco.org/profiles/EN/EDU/)

Source: UIS website, Statistics in Brief, Education in Jamaica.

In secondary education we see the beginnings of a slight disparity in NER, with boys falling three percentage points behind girls both in 1990/1991 and 2002/2003 (Table 8). The most recent GPI of 2002/2003 for secondary education stands at 1.04. Statistics from the *EFA Global Monitoring Report 2006* that show the percentage of repeaters in secondary general education, however, suggest a deeper problem, with boys more than twice as likely to repeat in 2002/2003 than girls (2.3 per cent for boys and 0.8 per cent for girls) (UNESCO, 2005).[14]

## TABLE 8: ENROLMENT RATIOS IN SECONDARY EDUCATION, JAMAICA

| SECONDARY | | 1990/ 1991 | 1998/ 1999 | 2000/ 2001 | 2002/ 2003 | REGIONAL AVERAGE 2002/2003 |
|---|---|---|---|---|---|---|
| GROSS ENROLMENT RATIO (GER) (%) | MF | 65 | 84 | 83 | 84 | 88 |
| | M | 64 | 83 | 82 | 83 | 85 |
| | F | 67 | 85 | 85 | 85 | 91 |
| NET ENROLMENT RATIO (NER) (%) | MF | 64 | 79 | 74 | 75 | 66 |
| | M | 62 | 78 | 73 | 74 | 64 |
| | F | 65 | 80 | 76 | 77 | 68 |

Notes:   (a) Regional refers to the entire Caribbean.
(b) Some data cover specific years or are an estimate. See the UIS website for more information.

Source: UIS website, Statistics in Brief, Education in Jamaica.

14   Statistical Annex, Table 8, p 339.

It is at the tertiary level, however, that the disparity becomes more apparent (Table 9). Female students have gone from being behind males in 1990/1991 to being more than twice as likely to enter college as their male counterparts in 2002/2003. Post-secondary non-tertiary education is also mainly female at 59 per cent of the total. What we see indicated here is an issue of either underperformance by boys when compared with their female counterparts that disallows them from accessing tertiary education, or a chosen path away from higher education.

TABLE 9: GROSS ENROLMENT RATIO (GER) IN TERTIARY EDUCATION, JAMAICA

| TERTIARY | | 1990/ 1991 | 1998/ 1999 | 2000/ 2001 | 2002/ 2003 | REGIONAL AVERAGE 2002/2003 |
|---|---|---|---|---|---|---|
| | MF | 7 | ... | 16 | 17 | 26 |
| GER (%) | M | 8 | ... | 11 | 10 | 24 |
| | F | 6 | ... | 22 | 25 | 28 |

Notes:  (a) Regional refers to the entire Caribbean.
(b) Some data cover specific years or are an estimate. See the UIS website for more information.

Source: UIS website, Statistics in Brief, Education in Jamaica.

A closer look is therefore needed at the details of boys' performance in formal education in order to understand the scope of their fall behind girls at the later secondary levels and the subsequent lower numbers that transition to both non-tertiary and tertiary education. For example, the Youth Literacy Rate for 2000-2004 (ages 15-24) showed a GPI of 1.07.[15] Statistics available from the Jamaican Ministry of Education on the performance of boys and girls in the June 2005 Caribbean Secondary Education Certificate (CSEC) examinations offered by the Caribbean Examinations Council (CXC) demonstrates more clearly where girls are outperforming boys in terms of subjects (Table 10).

The table outlines by gender the number of students who sat each subject, and reveals that more girls are entered for 29 of the 35 subjects listed, with the six exceptions all being technical/vocational courses (building tech – construction, building tech – woods, electrics and electronic tech, mechanical engineering tech, technical drawing and visual arts). Overall, only 48,992 boys sat the exams

---

15   Statistical Annex Table 12, UNESCO, 2006, p 387.

TABLE 10: PERFORMANCE OF JAMAICAN SECONDARY SCHOOL STUDENTS IN THE CSEC AT GENERAL & TECHNICAL PROFICIENCY LEVELS BY SEX, 2005

| SUBJECT | TOTAL | NO. MALE ENTRIES | NO. MALES GRADE 1-3 | % MALES GR. 1-3 | NO. FEMALE ENTRIES | NO. FEMALES GRADE 1-3 | % FEMALES GR. 1-3 |
|---|---|---|---|---|---|---|---|
| **ARTS** | | | | | | | |
| CARIBBEAN HISTORY | 5,101 | 1,621 | 959 | 59.2 | 3,480 | 2,168 | 62.3 |
| ENGLISH A | 19,956 | 7,654 | 4,011 | 52.4 | 12,302 | 7,995 | 65.0 |
| ENGLISH B | 6,917 | 1,885 | 1,075 | 57.0 | 5,032 | 3,491 | 69.4 |
| FRENCH | 592 | 182 | 123 | 67.6 | 410 | 286 | 69.8 |
| GEOGRAPHY | 3,728 | 1,792 | 1,008 | 56.3 | 1,936 | 1,121 | 57.9 |
| MUSIC | 77 | 34 | 22 | 64.7 | 43 | 32 | 74.4 |
| RELIGIOUS EDUCATION | 2,211 | 877 | 649 | 74.0 | 1,334 | 1,086 | 81.4 |
| SOCIAL STUDIES | 10,484 | 3,803 | 2,801 | 73.7 | 6,681 | 5,314 | 79.5 |
| SPANISH | 3,077 | 717 | 447 | 62.3 | 2,360 | 1,491 | 63.2 |
| **SCIENCES** | | | | | | | |
| BIOLOGY | 4,661 | 1,545 | 941 | 60.9 | 3,116 | 1,950 | 62.6 |
| CHEMISTRY | 3,597 | 1,436 | 722 | 50.3 | 2,161 | 1,142 | 52.8 |
| INTEGRATED SCIENCE | 4,914 | 1,853 | 1,314 | 70.9 | 3,061 | 2,226 | 72.7 |
| MATHEMATICS | 15,958 | 6,551 | 2,595 | 39.6 | 9,407 | 3,690 | 39.2 |
| PHYSICS | 3,071 | 1,640 | 906 | 55.2 | 1,431 | 918 | 64.2 |
| **TECHNICAL/VOCATIONAL** | | | | | | | |
| AGRI. SCIENCE (DOUBLE AWARD) | 358 | 133 | 120 | 90.2 | 225 | 209 | 92.9 |
| AGRI. SCIENCE (SINGLE AWARD) ANIMAL SCIENCE | 676 | 263 | 188 | 71.5 | 413 | 313 | 75.8 |
| AGRI. SCIENCE (SINGLE AWARD) CROPS & SOIL | 946 | 376 | 255 | 67.8 | 570 | 348 | 61.1 |
| BUILDING TECH: CONSTR. | 462 | 418 | 331 | 79.2 | 44 | 35 | 79.5 |
| BUILDING TECH: WOODS | 818 | 786 | 221 | 28.1 | 32 | 6 | 18.8 |
| CLOTHING & TEXTILES | 1,115 | 65 | 47 | 72.3 | 1,050 | 863 | 82.2 |
| ELEC. DOC. PREP. & MGMT. | 814 | 158 | 127 | 80.4 | 656 | 599 | 91.3 |
| ELECT. & ELECTRONIC TECH. | 1,786 | 1,690 | 837 | 49.5 | 96 | 52 | 54.2 |
| FOOD & NUTRITION | 3,523 | 484 | 374 | 77.3 | 3,039 | 2,618 | 86.1 |
| HOME ECONOMICS | 2,837 | 292 | 246 | 84.2 | 2,545 | 2,266 | 89.0 |
| HUMAN & SOCIAL BIOLOGY | 2,627 | 737 | 231 | 31.3 | 1,890 | 605 | 32.0 |
| INFORMATION TECHNOLOGY | 6,545 | 2,530 | 1,772 | 70.0 | 4,015 | 2,744 | 68.3 |
| MECH. ENG. TECH. | 818 | 787 | 324 | 41.2 | 31 | 13 | 41.9 |
| PHYS. ED. & SPORTS | 44 | 22 | 19 | 86.4 | 22 | 19 | 86.4 |
| TECHNICAL DRAWING | 2,569 | 2,327 | 1,169 | 50.2 | 242 | 140 | 57.9 |
| THEATRE ARTS | 212 | 50 | 41 | 82.0 | 162 | 145 | 89.5 |
| VISUAL ARTS | 1,685 | 974 | 634 | 65.1 | 711 | 426 | 59.9 |
| **BUSINESS** | | | | | | | |
| OFFICE PROCEDURES | 3,715 | 973 | 824 | 84.7 | 2,742 | 2,341 | 85.4 |
| PRINCIPLES OF ACCOUNTS | 6,408 | 1,959 | 1,314 | 67.1 | 4,449 | 3,156 | 70.9 |
| PRINCIPLES OF BUSINESS | 7,366 | 2,296 | 1,774 | 77.3 | 5,070 | 3,737 | 73.7 |
| TYPEWRITING | 435 | 82 | 41 | 50.0 | 353 | 162 | 45.9 |

*Source: Policy Analysis, Research and Statistics Unit, 2006.*

compared to 81,111 girls. This alone is a strong indicator of high drop-out rates among boys and disparity in survival to the final stages of formal education.

A further analysis of the data reveals that not only are the absolute numbers of girls receiving Grades 1-3 in these subjects much higher overall than those of boys as a result of higher entries, but also the percentage of Grades 1-3 among those girls who sat the exam is consistently higher than boys in most subjects with the exception of mathematics and a few technical/ vocational subjects and business. Again with the exception of mathematics, girls outperform boys in all of the sciences (traditionally thought of as male topics) and even perform better in those subjects where significantly more boys entered the exam, such as technical drawing. It is, however, in the arts that girls clearly outperform boys in both the number of entries and the final results, and particularly in English. For example, in English A we see 12,302 female entries compared to 7,654 male entries, with 12.6 per cent more girls achieving a Grade 1-3 than boys. Cumulatively, this does not bode well for the numbers of boys leaving school with sufficient English literacy.

However, it is important to place these statistics within a broader context that shows certain complexities. For example, if we look at employment data in Jamaica, we see a distinct gender advantage in terms of male employment as opposed to female employment. The 2004 unemployment rate for males stood at 8.1 compared to females at 15.7, and in terms of active job seeking, only 4.5 per cent of males were looking for work as opposed to 8.4 per cent of females.[16] Putting this data together with that showing boys underperforming in more subjects than girls and therefore less likely to transition to further/ higher education can lead to either of two interpretations: either (a) boys are being forced/ expected to enter into employment as a result of several possible reasons, such as their poorer performance in formal schooling and a variety of other social and economic factors; or (b) girls may have no option but to continue in education due to societal bias within the employment sector in favour of males. The reality is that either of these possibilities is detrimental to the overall developmental growth of males and females if the principles of gender equality are to be upheld, while society in the long run will inevitably suffer for it.

---

16   Statistical Institute of Jamaica, Jamaican Labour Force Statistics. Data available at: www.statinja.com/stats.html

# SITUATIONAL CONTEXT

The stratified nature of the Jamaican educational structure explains to some extent the high drop-out rates occurring at senior secondary level. Secondary departments in All-Age, Primary and Junior High Schools, which account for nearly 16 per cent of secondary school enrolment, do not currently go beyond Grade 9 and thus do not offer upper secondary education. It is after this point that there is a quick fall in enrolment, partly due to this lack of upper secondary school facilities. This situation is particularly problematic for rural schools with small catchment populations, and for poorer students who find it difficult to bear the costs associated with continuing education in a school located far from home. However, it is not clear why this particular structural feature affects boys more negatively than girls.

The literature review in Chapter 2 documented perspectives that showed Jamaica as a society where male privilege is widespread. However, while this patriarchal advantage allowed boys to outperform girls in the past, it is now suggested that as girls' access to education is increased, the impact of a narrow and potentially redundant masculinity on boys is hampering their achievement within the educational system.

> *...it is now suggested that as girls' access to education is increased, the impact of a narrow and potentially redundant masculinity on boys is hampering their achievement within the educational system.*

We have seen that one of the more serious problems is students' literacy and reading abilities. Poor reading abilities tend to be concentrated among boys. Because of their reading deficiency, they cannot learn the content of various subjects. This is a paradox of Jamaican education that standard statistics may not clearly reveal: high enrolment rates through to lower secondary, coupled with low learning that could be hampered by decreasing interest and participation. The literature suggests a selection of reasons behind this increasing lack of interest and participation on the part of boys. A popular perspective within the country is that of the 'spoiling' of young boys who are raised under the Jamaican notion of 'tie the heifer and loose the bull': i.e., that a girl should be regularly supervised and given tasks to do in the house, while a boy should be allowed to do as he pleases. Rooted within a concept of masculinity that is now working negatively against boys in terms of their academic performance, the outcomes of this socialisation could be manifesting themselves among some boys through alienation from the values of high academic achievement and the school system.

A study of male underachievement opens the door for an examination of the ways in which both boys and girls are prevented from achieving. Thus while males may be dominant within the wider society, they achieve less than girls within the schools, and choose less frequently than girls to continue their education. Schools can reflect the values of the wider society, and teachers are not immune to the norms and expectations that the society has for each sex. The practices of streaming and exclusion of some students from activities for arbitrary reasons are examples of school structures and/or teacher expectations that can lead to differences in participation and achievement. Therefore, while the statistics may show gender parity in primary school enrolment and transition and only a slight gender disparity at secondary level, there could be an attitudinal problem that starts quite early within the system but is more difficult to identify, as pointed out by Evans (1999) in her study on Jamaica:

> ...boys and girls enter Grade 1 in equal numbers and with roughly the same kinds of experiences and skills, though we know nothing about their attitudes to school work at this age. ...By the time they reached Grade 5 and 6, major distinctions were detectable in their attitude to and interest in work, the quality of work which they produced and in the academic performance.... In many of the schools, the streaming decisions made at the Grade 3 and 4 level influenced the students' CEE chances for the remainder of the primary years. By Grade 5 boys were over-represented in the low streams according to the reports of the teachers... [and] we conclude that the primary school contributes to this differential socialization.

## AN INNOVATIVE APPROACH ADOPTED BY SEVEN INNER-CITY SCHOOLS

Jamaican educators are now realising the need to adopt more holistic approaches. This report will now look at a project that has aimed to tackle these issues through experience sharing, teacher commitment and designing specific initiatives for each of the schools that adopted the project. The first part describes the methodology and programme development of the project, and the second highlights the response of a particular school to the innovations used.

## The 'Change from Within' programme

'Change from Within' (CFW) is a programme of human resource development involving a partnership among schools, communities, organisations and the larger society. The project was initially instituted by a former Vice Chancellor of the University of the West Indies (UWI), the late Sir Philip Sherlock, who brought together four schools that, independently of one another, were trying various ways of dealing with essentially the same problems of increasing violence and anti-social behaviour among boys. CFW took the shape of an applied research project where Sir Philip led a team of UWI scholars to find ways of building the self-esteem of students, which in his opinion lay at the root of the problems. Sharing ideas, participating in workshops and networking among the teachers were the main activities encouraged at that time, during which the programme expanded from four to seven schools. The methodology developed on the basis of analysis of work being done in these schools by the UWI team helped in a later expansion to 32 schools. The project demonstrated how CFW could become a powerful liberating force, building self-esteem and pride in one's ancestry and in the African-Jamaican record of historic achievements.

### *The Circle of Friends*

The designated 'engine' of the programme was the Circle of Friends, a leadership programme where school principals met together with a few support staff and a research team. The purpose was to tackle difficult issues around the education of boys and develop actions/ solutions. They shared experiences and ideas, planned strategies for action and learnt how to improve leadership skills. The eight meetings that were held were central to CFW's participatory methodology and facilitated effective feedback and communicative planning. The group's meetings allowed for the adjustments of strategies depending on how different schools identified their problems. This meant that changes could be made to procedures depending on the circumstances that existed. There was always a certain amount of openness and willingness to respond to feedback and the experiences of others.

These meetings helped the participants to draw on others' rich experiences and a large knowledge base generated by other research findings across different schools. CFW thus is all about self-help and capacity building. As members of the group met regularly, shared with each other and grappled with the challenges before them, they developed a close network. They grew as a committed and dedicated team that not only made comments and suggestions about what was happening

*It was found that individual styles and differences were less important when there was 'representativeness', a problem-solving focus and a recognition of the importance of the principles of commitment, shared vision and openness to learning.*

at the schools, but also provided emotional and psychological support to each other.

As group members were faced with the challenge of mobilising participants at a number of different levels, it became clear that effective leadership requires a set of important qualities. Some of these are shared vision, commitment, team approach, problem solving/ conflict reduction skills, openness to learning, and the ability to provide mutual support and help manage the distress and challenges of change. It was observed that within this group members had different styles, approaches, capabilities and skills. What was important, however, was the recognition that leadership was about dealing with a particular reality and building a process of adaptive change in relation to that reality.

Participants were also encouraged to recognise that for organisations to change in a serious way, the people in those organisations also had to change and must do so by recognising and responding to the adaptive challenges facing them. The Circle of Friends as a leadership collective represented various levels of progress and allowed these representatives to work together on problem solving, drawing together all of the available resources to ensure sustainable solutions. It was found that individual styles and differences were less important when there was 'representativeness', a problem-solving focus and a recognition of the importance of the principles of commitment, shared vision and openness to learning.

### The CFW methodology

The methodology of the CFW programme operated at a number of different levels. First, a participatory action research strategy was adopted that involved the engagement of all the stakeholders: the community, the students, the teachers, the administration and the parents. The main activities included observation, documentation, discussion and analysis.

At another level, the methodology also adopted a number of strategies for promoting change and building cooperation within and between schools. These involved:

i  creating a general awareness of the process;

ii  building social skills;

iii  establishing positive interdependence; and

iv  encouraging supportiveness and building a good interpersonal environment.

Positive interactions were promoted to create a climate that built morale and self esteem and encouraged respect, trust and conflict reduction. The methodology also included the process of institution building, 'servicing the infrastructure' to encourage self help. Workshops, training sessions and meetings served not only to provide guidance and assistance, but also to encourage the participants to identify and own the problems and challenges within their respective schools, generate workable solutions, map plans for action and implement strategies.

The programme development involved articulating the significant activities planned within the different schools. These activities specifically related to the challenges the respective schools had identified. The following list from one school provides an indication:

i    parental support and involvement in school activities;

ii   engagement of the communities;

iii  use of self expression and the arts as a means for self improvement, communication and motivation;

iv   guidance and counselling programmes as a means for identifying and solving personal problems;

v    bad behaviour seen as a cry for help;

vi   curriculum rooted in the cultural identity needs of Jamaicans;

vii  sensitivity to the particular needs of male students;

viii highly trained teaching staff who are committed to the change process;

ix   efficient and effective management techniques and practices/ ownership by the key stakeholders as a result of consultation and analysis of needs;

x    leadership prepared to take risks;

xi   recognising the need to develop emotional intelligence for children.

Through a series of school-based action research projects, two factors were identified that contributed to the alienation of boys: (a) the nature of boys' early socialisation by their parents, community and school; and (b) the 'drill to kill' teaching and learning methods that increasingly have marginalised boys and many girls from the schooling process. CFW identified four key challenges in the development of boys and young men in Jamaican society:

1    A lack of self esteem among young boys. Many children, because of their cultural and material environment, can develop a sense of worthlessness.

2    The growing problem of violence and the lack of discipline in schools and communities. This was highlighted by recent severe acts of violence

within at least three secondary schools that were part of the project.

3 Gender performance in school. This involved the way in which masculine identities work within the current environment, often moving boys away from academic performance and towards other compensatory but more negative types of behaviour.

4 The nature of the current socio-economic environment and the limited opportunities for jobs after students graduate. Alternative lifestyles – often outside of acceptable values and good citizenry – were therefore seen as more attractive.

The important lesson learnt at this point was that there was no one method for promoting CFW; rather, it was an evolving process that operated at different levels. Individual schools responded to local peculiarities in different ways and were able to promote CFW by pursuing their chosen objectives and working with different visions. A matrix of change was developed working on four levels – individual, school, parents/ home and wider community – that schools and policy makers could use as a school improvement tool to raise the achievement of boys. Schools' experiences revealed that 'active learning' and radical ways of engaging parents in the education of their children were producing positive outcomes.

Over the year 2001-2002, CFW identified a set of common principles that guided the activities in the seven schools involved in the project at that time. They were generated out of the challenges identified within the schools and the approaches utilised to dealing with these challenges. These principles constitute the methodology of the CFW:

- empowering school leaders: leaders, being different from managers, have a vision, are ready to take risks, are approachable and also capable of empowering others.

- working on the positives – good practice: identification of areas such as sports and performing arts where success brings kudos and following up with positive feedback and creating a culture of striving for better performance and success.

- a new pedagogy: immediate environment being used as a learning resource allowing for debates and collaborative learning.

- mentoring: taking the responsibility for overall development of students and not limiting it to learning of specific skills or building particular kinds of knowledge.

- involvement of parents and the wider community: parents becoming part of the school community, involving themselves in decision-making, helping in co-curricular activities and even evincing concern over the welfare of the teachers.

- involvement of students: consultation and communication with students, allowing them to be represented in decision-making through democratic channels based on well-defined norms.

- circle of support: developing a culture of sharing without fear or being judgemental, and learning from each other.

## Blue Mountain High School[17]

Blue Mountain High School had been one of Jamaica's prestigious schools and in the past had educated the country's elite. However, that image had changed as the school started taking children from poorer backgrounds and faced problems of violence, gang-culture, drug addiction and underperformance. As part of the CFW project, the principal introduced certain interventions that focused on changing the basic quests of boys in conforming to the stereotypical gender identity and helping them develop a worldview that would go beyond themselves. The case study of the school is based on discussions with the principal, teachers, the guidance counsellor, parents and students as well as on participation in a number of school activities. Two such programmes were a series of workshops on parenting skills and a CFW residential summer camp.

### *Problems and challenges*

The school was confronted by some of the common problems experienced by a number of inner-city schools in Jamaica. These included inter-school rivalry and conflict, student indiscipline and insecurity stemming from poor family relations, low level of teacher motivation and commitment, non-facilitative internal structures and procedures, 'cliquism' among teachers and lack of effective staff development programmes. The principal stated that when he first took up the position, he made a list of the problems and challenges facing the school as he saw it. He adopted a formal yet decentralised approach to leadership and designed an evaluation system for assessing success in changing the school.

---

17. The name of school has been changed to protect the identity of the school, teachers and students.

Increasing incidents of violence carried out by students of the school within and outside its premises were a major concern. An emergency response team, comprised of teachers and community representatives, was formed to deal directly with this problem and covered violence both on the streets and on the school compound. Also, a ban was instituted on cellular phone use, weapons and any instrument that could be used to inflict injury. The school rule was very clear and stringent in relation to weapons violations. The use of metal detectors was introduced in an attempt to eradicate weapon use at the school.

Identifying and tracking down gangs was not easy, and boys were included in the gangs from an early age. Teachers used the occasions of fights, inter-school altercations and stabbing injuries to identify the students and trace others. A First Grade teacher reported that she had identified at least two students in her class who sometimes did not come to lessons but hid in the bushes behind the school to smoke with older boys of a particular gang.

According to the principal, the strict measures against violence coupled with other measures have helped the school to almost completely eradicate gangs. Feedback from other sources suggests that the problem has not been wiped out altogether, but it has definitely been reduced.

### The effective use of counselling services

The school introduced guidance counselling services and used them successfully to help students deal with various kinds of emotional problems. For instance, a boy faced extreme anger from his mother for bad performance and was humiliated by her in front of his teacher and peers. It was a volatile situation where he could have reacted violently, making the situation worse. The principal, teacher and counsellor together worked on restoring his confidence, and subsequent counselling sessions helped him to deal with the situation well. Counselling also greatly helped students after two separate accidents in which several students attending the school died. Many students, especially those who had lost their friends, were miserable and counselling helped them overcome their grief.

The shock of these deaths was also used to pull students away from violence and express themselves through various other means. The boys were encouraged to show their emotions, cry and not feel that seeking care was 'unmanly' and therefore unacceptable. This helped them change their image of appropriate male identity, making it more rounded. Counselling, coupled with participation in a number of decisions that the management was taking about school administration, also made students trust the teachers and school staff in general and feel a sense of ownership of the school. Corporal punishment was strictly banned and that too made students feel more secure and cared for. As a result of these measures, students starting interacting better with teachers and participating in school activities more openly and willingly. Given the family background of most boys in this school, with many of them coming from single-parent households and lacking care and attention at home, the support from school was important. It had a positive impact on their attendance as well as their performance.

*...with strong leadership and appropriate strategies, schools can make a difference even in situations that appear to be most difficult and daunting.*

One of the limitations witnessed in the school was that the experiences have not been integrated into main curricular practices and most classes continued to follow the traditional lecture format, with little space for student expression through various means. There was no evidence of children's work on the walls, the classrooms were dark and bleak, and outside of sports the boys had few outlets to channel their emotions and creativity.

# CONCLUSIONS

The case study of this school within the frame of the CFW project shows that, with strong leadership and appropriate strategies, schools can make a difference even in situations that appear to be most difficult and daunting. Within the school a set of strong rules coupled with measures that encouraged more participation helped students change their attitude and behaviour, indicating that strict rules can be effective if they are implemented in the right mix. The school functioned within a project that promoted sharing, cooperation, mutual learning, experimentation and continuous growth, breaking its isolation and inertia. The same principles were applied in strategies adopted at school level that helped in reducing the boys' alienation from school and education processes. The school focused on management-related reforms and succeeded in bringing about change to a large extent. It is also clear, however, that the change would be more sustainable and effective if these reforms were combined with pedagogical reforms based on similar principles, as was apparently evidenced in some other schools that were part of the project.

# 6.

# Lesotho: a case of under-participation

## THE MACRO-LEVEL PICTURE

Lesotho is one of the few developing countries where gender disparities have been noticed in favour of girls in schooling participation rates and educational outcomes, though the country is far from reaching universalisation even for the primary stage of education. These disparities exist in literacy rates as well as participation rates at both primary and secondary stages. The participation rates for both boys and girls are low at secondary stage. However, within this situation of low participation, the enrolment rates are still lower for boys (Table 11). In fact, gender gaps are higher at the secondary stage of education indicating a lower survival rate or higher drop-out rate for boys in the post-primary phase of schooling. In this context, it is also important to remember that Lesotho, a small, landlocked country located in Southern Africa, has a total population of 2 million; hence even small change in numbers lead to significant changes in percentage terms. Nevertheless, there is no denying the fact that there is a clear case of boys' under-participation.

TABLE 11: SELECTED EDUCATIONAL INDICATORS, LESOTHO (PERCENTAGES)

| | YEAR | TOTAL | MALE | FEMALE | GENDER PARITY INDEX (GPI) FEMALES/ MALES |
|---|---|---|---|---|---|
| ADULT LITERACY RATE | 1990 | 78.0 | 65.4 | 89.5 | 1.37 |
| | 2000-2004 | 81.4 | 73.7 | 90.3 | 1.22 |
| NET ENROLMENT RATIO (NER) AT PRIMARY STAGE | 1998-1999 | 64.5 | 60.3 | 68.7 | 1.14 |
| | 2002-2003 | 85.8 | 82.9 | 88.6 | 1.07 |
| NET ENROLMENT RATIO (NER) AT SECONDARY STAGE | 1998-1999 | 14.0 | 9.7 | 18.3 | 1.89 |
| | 2002-2003 | 22.5 | 17.8 | 27.2 | 1.53 |

*Source: UNESCO, 2006.*

The trends are not as clear in the case of under-performance, the other aspect of boys' underachievement. The results of the Southern and Eastern Consortium for Monitoring Educational Quality II (SACMEQ II) 2000-2002 shows that there is hardly any difference between boys and girls in reading literacy in Lesotho (Figure 1). SACMEQ II was the first time Lesotho had participated in the survey (which originated in Zimbabwe in 1991), and the reading and mathematics achievements of Grade 6 were assessed on a sample basis.

Interestingly, the region presents a variety of gender patterns: while girls are clearly performing better than boys in some countries such as Botswana, Mauritius, Seychelles, South Africa, Swaziland and Uganda, the opposite is true in Kenya, Mozambique and United Republic of Tanzania, and still others – Lesotho, Malawi, Namibia and Zambia – depict insignificant differences. The countries showing insignificant differences are usually the low achievers as well.

## FIGURE 1: GENDER DISPARITIES IN READING LITERACY IN SUB-SAHARAN AFRICAN COUNTRIES

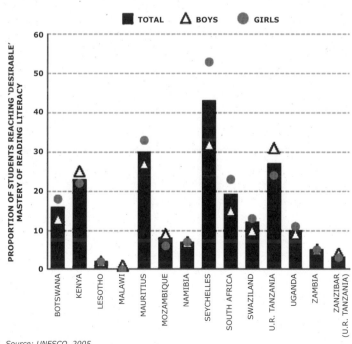

*Source: UNESCO, 2005*

Boys and girls in Lesotho show similar scores despite the fact that repetition rates are higher for boys in all zones (Table 12). According to a government report (Government of Lesotho, 2000), girls perform better than boys in all the grades at the primary education level, but the scores for both sexes level off in the final examinations. What is obviously more worrisome for Lesotho is the fact that it has one of the lowest levels of proficiency for both boys and girls among all the countries that participated in SAQMEC II.

### TABLE 12: PERCENTAGE OF PUPILS WHO ARE REPEATERS, LESOTHO

| ECOLOGICAL ZONE | FEMALE | MALE | TOTAL |
|---|---|---|---|
| FOOTHILLS | 16 | 22 | 19 |
| LOWLANDS | 14 | 20 | 17 |
| MOUNTAIN | 18 | 23 | 20 |
| SENGU RIVER VALLEY | 14 | 17 | 18 |
| **TOTAL** | 16 | 21 | 18 |

Source: Government of Lesotho and the World Bank, 2005.

The above analysis establishes that under-performance of both boys and girls is a major issue in Lesotho. However, boys deserve special attention on two counts: (a) the relative under-participation of boys in terms of enrolment in a situation where the participation of all children is low; and (b) boys' relatively higher repetition rate.

An important aspect of Lesotho society is that although slightly more girls attend school and consequently have higher literacy rates, this is neither the result of nor leads to better positioning of women. Despite impressive advances compared to some other sub-Saharan African countries, with significant representation of women in almost all sectors including administrative and managerial positions, unequal gender relations are still a dominant feature in Lesotho (Kimane et al, 1998; Abagi, 2003). The patrilineal and patriarchal system continues to subordinate women to men, and customary law classifies women as minors that need to be perpetually subjected to the guardianship of their male counterparts. Boys' under-participation, therefore, does not emanate from their secondary position, as had been the case with girls in most parts of the world. Rather, it has its roots in the age-old practice of herdboys tending livestock. Livestock are an important part of Lesotho traditions and boys are engaged in looking after them from a young age. The practice continues in rural areas, especially among the population living in the highlands.

About one third of Lesotho's population lives in the highlands, where villages are small and isolated, separated by steep mountains. The temperatures are cooler and snow falls during the winter months. Most families there raise animals such as sheep, cattle or angora goats. Livestock, apart from being a source of pride, are also one of the important sources of livelihood and nearly every boy spends part of his life as a herdboy. They pass their days in taking the family's herd to a field where they can graze and searching for new places where the animals can feed the next day. During winter this often means taking the herd to the fields a few miles from home. When spring planting begins, these young herdboys need to go further up into the mountains to look for pasturelands. As the demands of schooling clash with those of the livestock, these herdboys are one of the main groups that remain outside the fold of modern education.

*An important aspect of Lesotho society is that although slightly more girls attend school and consequently have higher literacy rates, this is neither the result of nor leads to better positioning of women.*

The practice can be associated with the traditional perception that wealth was counted in terms of the number of livestock a family had. Several researchers have pointed out that herding of animals is considered a good practice even in terms of socialising the male child to become a responsible member of family and society (Mokhosi et al, 1999). According to these researchers, the initiation to herding animals tends to begin between three and five years when young boys start accompanying their elder brothers or relatives to look after animals. Most herdboys come from poor family backgrounds. The situation is worse for children who serve other families as herdboys and stay with their employers, as they work for little remuneration and are denied all their basic rights.

Figure 2 lists the barriers that cause under-participation, as seen in a number of studies. It is important to understand that indifference towards education combines with the practice of herding and poverty to act as a constraint to participation in schooling. The fact that the practice of being a herdboy is now mostly found only among the poor shows that it is not only a cultural issue. It is probably the only major livelihood option for many poor families based in rural areas located in the highlands. Therefore, the practice continues even if it clashes with the demands of schooling and leads to a lack of formal education among boys. Studies also indicate that lack of education means lack of information about health-related issues, leading to a high prevalence of HIV/AIDS and drug abuse.

## FIGURE 2: OBSTACLES THAT CONTRIBUTE TO THE FAILURE TO ATTAIN A FORMAL EDUCATION, LESOTHO

| FACTOR | SUPPORTING STATEMENT/S |
|---|---|
| POVERTY/CONSTRAINTS | SCHOOL FEES, BOOK FEES, UNIFORMS, FEEDING SCHEME PLACE TOO HIGH DEMANDS ON THE MAJORITY OF PARENTS |
| CULTURAL PRACTICES | CULTURAL PERCEPTIONS, NEGATIVE PARENTAL ATTITUDES, PRACTICES SUCH AS INITIATIONS AND EARLY MARRIAGES AS WELL AS MISSING SCHOOL TO ATTEND TO HOUSEHOLD CHORES OR HERDING ANIMALS |
| SUBSTANCE ABUSE | YOUNG PERSONS ENGAGE IN DRUG ABUSE AND ALCOHOLISM |
| FACILITIES | LACK OF HEALTHY PHYSICAL AND SANITARY FACILITIES IN SCHOOLS, INCLUDING TOILETS AND DESKS |
| HEALTH | HIV/AIDS INFECTED AND AFFECTED, THE HIGH HIV/AIDS PREVALENCE AND MANY ORPHANED BOYS AND GIRLS |
| PREGNANCY | CASES OF TEENAGE PREGNANCY IN PRIMARY SCHOOLS, MORE SO THOSE IN RURAL AREAS |
| DISTANCE | LONG DISTANCES FROM SCHOOLS |
| NEGATIVE ATTITUDE | SCHOOL IS CONSIDERED TO BE AN UNNECESSARY ACTIVITY; PEOPLE ARE SOMETIMES SIMPLY TOO LAZY OR SHY TO ATTEND |
| CLASH IN SCHEDULE | HERDBOYS LEAVE EARLY IN THE MORNING, SPEND THE WHOLE DAY IN THE FIELD AND COME BACK IN THE EVENING |
| ERRATIC OR NON-ATTENDANCE | HERDBOYS ARE REQUIRED TO WORK ALL YEAR ROUND, A SITUATION THAT AFFECTS REGULAR ATTENDANCE |

*Source: Respondents, Odumbe, 1990; Gill, 1994; Mokhosi et al, 1999; Abagi, 2003; Makhetha and Motlomelo, 2004; Government of Lesotho and UNICEF, 1994.*

Even when herdboys and other children from poor families enrol in schools, the incidence of absenteeism remains high, affecting their continuation and performance. Although absenteeism is high among girls too, it is reportedly higher for boys. Fetching water is the main activity that leads to girls' absenteeism, but that appears to be less demanding in terms of conflicting with the school day as compared to being a herdboy. The isolated nature of villages, separated by mountains, also poses physical barriers in terms of attending schools. The lack of facilities makes schools in rural areas an unattractive option, and these areas face a paucity of teachers, especially qualified ones. The school census records school location in four general categories and, although this is not normally used for analysis, it was used by a study undertaken by the Government of Lesotho and the World Bank (2005). This reveals that 51 per cent of teachers in mountain areas are unqualified, compared with only 24 per cent in lowland areas (Table 13). Even these figures may mask greater teacher shortages in the most isolated schools, as many schools might not have any or only one qualified teacher. The study opines, "It is hard to attract people to rural areas, as the conditions are difficult… Young people, even those from rural areas, want to come down from the highlands as soon as they can". The high incidence of teacher absenteeism in rural areas for a variety of reasons compounds the problem.

*The lack of facilities makes schools in rural areas an unattractive option, and these areas face a paucity of teachers, especially qualified ones.*

TABLE 13: PERCENTAGE OF TEACHERS WHO ARE UNQUALIFIED BY LOCATION, LESOTHO

| ECOLOGICAL ZONE | FEMALE | MALE | TOTAL |
|---|---|---|---|
| FOOTHILLS | 35 | 58 | 39 |
| LOWLANDS | 21 | 39 | 24 |
| MOUNTAIN | 47 | 60 | 51 |
| SENQU RIVER VALLEY | 26 | 59 | 35 |

*Source: Government of Lesotho and the World Bank, 2005.*

Considering the mountainous nature of the terrain and the dispersed nature of the population, open and distance learning (ODL) assumes a special significance. This case study looks at the experience of Lesotho Distance Teaching Centre in this context. It examines the Learning Post programme, which aims to take basic education to students living in remote areas.

# THE LESOTHO DISTANCE TEACHING CENTRE

The Lesotho Distance Teaching Centre (LDTC) was established in 1972 as a department of the Ministry of Education and Training. Initially, the Centre was set up to address the needs of secondary education using ODL methods. The focus was on students who had not passed the final secondary education examinations. The literacy and numeracy section of the Centre, which is now the Centre for Basic Education, was established in 1977 to provide literacy and skills training. The basic premise for starting this section was that it was not possible for some sections of the society to attend school due to a variety of reasons. Despite the introduction of free primary schooling, this is not universal due to the practice of cattle rearing as well as the lack of faith in the relevance of education mentioned above. The Learning Post (LP) programme was intended to cater for illiterate and semi-literate learners, most of whom are herdboys. This case study is based on a desk review of existing evaluation reports of the programme as well as consultation with all kinds of stakeholders including learners, volunteers, parents and administrators associated with the programme.

## Learning Post programme: A flexible option for the underprivileged

One of the most important features of the Lesotho Distance Teaching Centre is flexibility, which helps herdboys and others facing similar constraints. The

*One of the most important features of the Lesotho Distance Teaching Centre is flexibility, which helps herdboys and others facing similar constraints.*

LP programme offers learners the opportunity to complete the course at their own pace and in their own time. The hope of better employment opportunities and developing the capacity to deal with the exploitation that they often face were major motivations for learners joining the programme. Those who had dropped out of the formal system shared their experiences of not feeling comfortable there because of their age being higher than other students and lack of attention from teachers. This reflected that the formal system is not geared to deal with the specific needs of children from disadvantaged backgrounds.

A perusal of the family backgrounds of learners consulted reveals that they largely came from uneducated and poor households. The majority of parents had never been to school and remained illiterate. Almost all mothers were housewives and fathers were farmers, reflecting the fact that this programme was not a choice of those whose families were educated or in any kind of employment. The flexibility obviously helped poor children cope with the requirements of supporting their families and engaging in practices such as cattle grazing. There have been more male learners in the programme than female. Although not equivalent to primary education, the programme covers basic literacy and numeracy skills in addition to some vocational skills. All the respondents who were consulted stated that the LP programme has had a positive impact on the learners and their communities. Programme graduates have been actively participating in community-based development projects, and this was perceived as a good use of the skills acquired through the programme.

However, despite these positives, the LP programme has been questioned on several grounds. First of all, the learners do not complete a full cycle of primary or basic education and hence the programme cannot be considered as equivalent to the primary stage of schooling. This does not appear to be in conformity with the rights approach and can be viewed as a poor substitute for poor children, a criticism often made of alternatives that do not have the same or equivalent curricula. The present curriculum has also been questioned on the basis of relevance, and the need to include additional topics such as conflict resolution, HIV/AIDS, career guidance, basic criminology, etc has been highlighted. A number of respondents in the process of consultation suggested that the nature and quality of vocational skills needed to change if the learners were expected to use these to find employment. However, the recent decision to introduce the English language in the programme was viewed as a positive development by most of those consulted.

### Low paid but highly motivated teachers working in an un-enabling environment

The majority of the LP programme administrators/ teachers are middle-aged women. They serve as volunteers and receive monthly honoraria of about M150/ US$19. This low level of honoraria explains the disproportionate presence of women as men in general, and young men in particular, do not find it attractive enough. It also leads to a high incidence of turnover. However, the level of motivation among these administrators/ teachers is observed to generally be high, one of the major reasons that the quality of delivery has been acceptable despite adverse conditions. A number of these teachers had been associated with LDTC themselves and felt a sense of responsibility towards contributing to a programme that promotes literacy and education among the deprived. For instance, one of the teachers shared her experience of being able to complete her secondary schooling through an LDTC correspondence course, and noted that she finds this experience satisfying even if it is not rewarding in monetary terms. This sentiment was echoed by many other teachers as well. Nonetheless, it was also obvious in the process of consultation that motivation alone cannot sustain the programme, and a number of interventions are required to improve it further.

Lack of a conducive environment and of adequate facilities for schooling has been identified by a number of evaluations as a major obstacle in raising the quality of the LP programme. An enabling environment helps in attracting and retaining learners. The respondents, in particular the LP administrators, indicated that the schools' proprietors do not allow the programme administrators to use their facilities. This confirms the findings of almost all evaluations undertaken for LDTC, which have recommended the active involvement of stakeholders such as school proprietors, field-based education officers and parents or guardians in significant ways to improve the environment.

The LP programme relies heavily on the print and face-to-face mode of delivery. Evaluations suggest that reception of Radio Lesotho – which, among others, presents the language arts radio lesson programme – is on the whole good and have proposed that this facility might be one that can reach most learners and in particular herdboys. However, this would only be possible if the poor communities could be provided with radios. There appeared to be universal agreement that the use of modern technology would make the programme more accessible and cost-effective. This is especially relevant given the mountainous and remote nature of the terrain. It appeared that the LDTC does not use for training the radio slot provided by the Ministry of Education and Training, which has been in place for more than 20 years. Radio can be used creatively to teach a new language and thus has special relevance for the recent decision to teach English.

### Retention in the Learning Post programme

The retention rates are apparently not very high in the LP programme. Several reasons have been put forward for this. Primarily, it has to do with the herdboys' lifestyle. The boys who are employed tend to move from one employer to the other, and the new employer may not be in the same district or locality as the one in which the herdboy was able to participate in the programme. Even when they are not employed and herd their family's livestock, the sheer pressure of having worked through the day makes it difficult for them to come for these classes in the evening. Seasonality also affects attendance as boys tend to spend longer periods at the cattle post during winter while girls are retained at home for help during harvesting periods. In some cases, herdboys join circumcision school, after which they discontinue other forms of education. Early marriages are common and girls are often not permitted after marriage or pregnancy to go back to these classes. Makhetha and Motlomelo (2004) and UNICEF (2003) have also cited ill health, excessive drug abuse, attending to family chores such as working in the fields and lack of motivation as major causes of drop out from the programme. It is obvious that the whole issue of child labour needs to be addressed as these practices clash with any form of schooling. Language also acts as a barrier in some cases. Lesotho is largely homogenous and Sesotho is the main language and the medium of instruction. However, Xhosa and Zulu are also spoken in some parts.

# CONCLUSIONS

The case study shows that although ODL has potential as a solution in circumstances where the locations are remote and the population dispersed, it needs to be planned and implemented carefully if the objective is to provide basic or higher levels of education. A complete cycle of basic education cannot be treated as the same as literacy and requires the participation of children for longer hours on a sustained basis. ODL models can be successful only if they implement well-designed curricula using a variety of technological tools in combination with face-to-face interactions, which does not seem to be happening in this case. While the programme has provided literacy skills to a large number of herdboys who had either dropped out or never been to school, there remains the need for developing other solutions to the whole issue of boys' under-participation, which appears to be result of a combination of economic, social and physical factors in Lesotho.

*ODL models can be successful only if they implement well-designed curricula using a variety of technological tools in combination with face-to-face interactions...*

# 7.

# Samoa: a major challenge to the education system

Samoa is a low middle-income country with a small population of less than a million. It consists of eight islands in the Pacific – two large and six small – and has a single system of societal organisation and language. The country identifies

*Samoa... identifies boys' underachievement as a major challenge facing its education system.*

boys' underachievement as a major challenge facing its education system. This piece discusses the nature of the problem, followed by the analysis of a vocational education initiative that is viewed as having helped in addressing the issue.

## THE NATURE OF BOYS' UNDERACHIEVEMENT

A perusal of Tables 14 and 15 suggests that girls and boys are almost at par in terms of participation at the primary stage of schooling. Table 14 indicates that girls were at a slight disadvantage as compared to boys till the beginning of this century when the trend changed in their favour. However, the latest data for 2004 shows parity, and the gap on either side has not been significant. But the story is different for the secondary level of education. Participation rates have consistently been higher for girls, the gap being quite significant and somewhat widening over time. Participation rates for girls remain low, generally less than

50 per cent during the period 1995-2004, but the rates for boys are lower. In other words, boys have lower participation rates within a scenario of low overall participation at the secondary level.

## TABLE 14: PERCENTAGE PRIMARY NET ENROLMENT RATIO, 5-14-YEAR-OLDS, 1995-2004, SAMOA

| | 1995 | 1996 | 1997 | 1998 | 1999 | 2000 | 2001 | 2002 | 2003 | 2004 |
|---|---|---|---|---|---|---|---|---|---|---|
| MALE | 87 | 86 | 86 | 86 | 85 | 87 | 81 | 83 | 84 | 85 |
| FEMALE | 87 | 84 | 84 | 84 | 83 | 85 | 83 | 85 | 85 | 85 |
| TOTAL | 87 | 85 | 85 | 85 | 84 | 86 | 82 | 84 | 84.5 | 85 |

*Source: Ministry of Education, Sports and Culture, 2004c.*

## TABLE 15: PERCENTAGE SECONDARY NET ENROLMENT RATIO, 15-19-YEAR-OLDS, 1995-2004, SAMOA

| | 1995 | 1996 | 1997 | 1998 | 1999 | 2000 | 2001 | 2002 | 2003 | 2004 |
|---|---|---|---|---|---|---|---|---|---|---|
| MALE | 33 | 34 | 34 | 35 | 37 | 35 | 37 | 35 | 39 | 38 |
| FEMALE | 39 | 39 | 42 | 41 | 45 | 40 | 45 | 43 | 51 | 48 |
| TOTAL | 36 | 36 | 37 | 38 | 41 | 38 | 41 | 39 | 44 | 43 |

*Source: Ministry of Education, Sports and Culture, 2004c.*

Examinations results are analysed next to see whether under-participation of boys is also coupled with underperformance. Taking into account the examination structure followed by the national system, four examinations results are used here as measures of educational performance. These are the Samoa Primary Education Literacy Level (SPELL) One test for Year 4, the SPELL Two test for Year 6 and the National Year 12 Examination. At primary school level, the SPELL Tests for Years 4 and 6 were established and designed to identify and monitor students who are not achieving minimum competencies in both literacy and numeracy in schools. The results are recorded as an 'at-risk percentage' across government schools. Most non-government schools also participate.

Tables 16 and 17 show that a significantly higher proportion of boys have been at risk at the end of Year 4 as well as Year 6 in comparison to girls for all three subjects that are covered at this stage: English, Samoan and numeracy.

The situation is not encouraging for either girls or boys but it seems that boys
are particularly weak in English and numeracy, more than two thirds having
been identified as being at risk at the end of the Year 6 examinations.

TABLE 16: PERCENTAGE OF PRIMARY STUDENTS
IDENTIFIED AS AT RISK, YEAR 4, SAMOA

| SUBJECT | GENDER | 1998 | 1999 | 2000 | 2001 | 2002 | 2003 | 2004 |
|---------|--------|------|------|------|------|------|------|------|
| ENGLISH | BOYS   | 37   | 37   | 29   | 18   | 55   | 61   | 19   |
|         | GIRLS  | 22   | 20   | 17   | 11   | 41   | 41   | 8    |
|         | TOTAL  | 29   | 28   | 23   | 15   | 48   | 51   | 13   |
| SAMOAN  | BOYS   | 49   | 50   | 40   | 26   | 40   | 39   | 39   |
|         | GIRLS  | 28   | 31   | 26   | 15   | 23   | 20   | 19   |
|         | TOTAL  | 31   | 40   | 33   | 21   | 32   | 29   | 28   |
| NUMERACY| BOYS   | 37   | 33   | 30   | 29   | 33   | 40   | 40   |
|         | GIRLS  | 24   | 22   | 24   | 19   | 24   | 25   | 25   |
|         | TOTAL  | 30   | 38   | 27   | 24   | 28   | 32   | 32   |

Source: Government of Samoa, 2005c.

TABLE 17: PERCENTAGE OF PRIMARY STUDENTS
IDENTIFIED AS AT RISK, YEAR 6, SAMOA

| SUBJECT | GENDER | 1998 | 1999 | 2000 | 2001 | 2002 | 2003 | 2004 |
|---------|--------|------|------|------|------|------|------|------|
| ENGLISH | BOYS   | 67   | 69   | 51   | 60   | 63   | 68   | 69   |
|         | GIRLS  | 44   | 48   | 35   | 36   | 38   | 42   | 44   |
|         | TOTAL  | 53   | 58   | 46   | 48   | 50   | 55   | 56   |
| SAMOAN  | BOYS   | 25   | 28   | 24   | 23   | 27   | 24   | 17   |
|         | GIRLS  | 8    | 10   | 11   | 10   | 11   | 7    | 12   |
|         | TOTAL  | 15   | 19   | 17   | 16   | 19   | 16   | 12   |
| NUMERACY| BOYS   | 70   | 69   | 66   | 61   | 68   | 77   | 76   |
|         | GIRLS  | 54   | 53   | 51   | 50   | 56   | 64   | 58   |
|         | TOTAL  | 61   | 60   | 58   | 56   | 62   | 71   | 67   |

Source: Government of Samoa, 2005c.

Given these trends at primary level, the results at the end of Year 8 do not come
as a surprise. Table 18 shows that in all subjects examined in 2001, 2002 and
2004, the boys' mean score has remained below the 50 per cent mark. Female
students on the other hand had their mean score above the national average
of 50 per cent at around 53 and 54 per cent in these years. This means that
though girls continue to outperform boys in all subjects including science and

mathematics, the disparities in mean scores are much less when compared to the Year 6 level. However, students' performance in the Year 8 National Examination is used to select those who will enter the top five government secondary schools. As such, these results in this examination are extremely important for their "progression and future educational opportunities" (ADB, 2003).

TABLE 18: NATIONAL YEAR 8 MEAN SCORE
RESULTS BY SUBJECT AND SEX, SAMOA

| SUBJECT | SEX | 2001 | 2002 | 2004 |
|---|---|---|---|---|
| **BASIC SCIENCE** | BOYS | 48 | 47 | 48 |
| | GIRLS | 53 | 54 | 53 |
| | TOTAL | 51 | 50 | 50 |
| **ENGLISH** | BOYS | 46 | 46 | 46 |
| | GIRLS | 54 | 55 | 54 |
| | TOTAL | 50 | 50 | 50 |
| **MATHEMATICS** | BOYS | 48 | 47 | 47 |
| | GIRLS | 53 | 53 | 52 |
| | TOTAL | 51 | 50 | 50 |
| **SAMOAN** | BOYS | 47 | 46 | 47 |
| | GIRLS | 54 | 54 | 54 |
| | TOTAL | 50 | 50 | 51 |
| **SOCIAL SCIENCE** | BOYS | 48 | 47 | 47 |
| | GIRLS | 53 | 54 | 53 |
| | TOTAL | 50 | 50 | 50 |

*Source: Ministry of Education, Sports and Culture: Examiner.*

Table 19 shows mean scores by subject and sex for Year 12 National Examinations for four years. Girls have either been outperforming or are at par with boys in most subjects. However, though the average scores of girls are higher in most subjects, the differences are not very great. What becomes important in the Samoan case is the fact that boys are facing both under-participation and underperformance, especially at secondary level. The signs of underperformance start early at primary level, and this feature distinguishes Samoa from many other countries that face the problem of boys' underachievement.

TABLE 19: NATIONAL YEAR 12 MEAN SCORE
RESULTS BY SUBJECT AND SEX, SAMOA

| SUBJECT | SEX | 2001 | 2002 | 2003 | 2004 |
|---|---|---|---|---|---|
| ACCOUNTING | BOYS | 50 | 52 | 50 | 44 |
| | GIRLS | 50 | 53 | 53 | 48 |
| ECONOMICS | BOYS | 52 | 53 | 52 | 46 |
| | GIRLS | 50 | 55 | 55 | 49 |
| ENGLISH | BOYS | 43 | 46 | 46 | 44 |
| | GIRLS | 49 | 51 | 51 | 50 |
| FOOD & NUTRITION | BOYS | 34 | 39 | 39 | NA |
| | GIRLS | 38 | 42 | 43 | NA |
| GEOGRAPHY | BOYS | 48 | 51 | 50 | 46 |
| | GIRLS | 49 | 51 | 50 | 48 |
| HISTORY | BOYS | 50 | 54 | 54 | 47 |
| | GIRLS | 53 | 55 | 55 | 49 |
| MATHEMATICS | BOYS | 47 | 51 | 48 | 46 |
| | GIRLS | 48 | 49 | 49 | 48 |
| PHYSICS | BOYS | 53 | 59 | 57 | 45 |
| | GIRLS | 56 | 57 | 57 | 50 |
| SAMOAN | BOYS | 42 | 44 | 42 | 45 |
| | GIRLS | 47 | 48 | 47 | 49 |
| SCIENCE | BOYS | 44 | 49 | 51 | NA |
| | GIRLS | 49 | 50 | 50 | NA |
| DESIGN TECHNOLOGY | BOYS | 35 | 40 | 39 | NA |
| | GIRLS | 41 | 36 | 44 | NA |
| BIOLOGY | BOYS | | 52 | 49 | 47 |
| | GIRLS | | 49 | 50 | 48 |
| CHEMISTRY | BOYS | | 63 | 58 | 60 |
| | GIRLS | | 58 | 57 | 51 |

*Source: Ministry of Education, Sports and Culture: Examiner.*

# POST-SECONDARY EDUCATION AND EMPLOYMENT

The census is responded to by citizens at all age levels, and thus it gives a view of historical social trends. An analysis of data from the census shows that boys' underachievement is a recent phenomenon and has helped in reducing the gender difference in educational achievement. The 2001 census asked respondents to identify levels of educational achievement, and the responses show that the gender split of those completing university has been progressively changing over time. Over 70 per cent of people 75+ who had completed university were males. The relative proportions trended together and 50 years later the gender proportions equalised in the population that is now 25-30 years old (Figure 3). This equalisation has since led to a reversal of achievement trends at the tertiary level, with the current younger generation of women accessing university much more than their male counterparts.

*An analysis of data from the census shows that boys' underachievement is a recent phenomenon and has helped in reducing the gender difference in educational achievement.*

FIGURE 3: GENDER OF INDIVIDUALS WHO HAVE COMPLETED UNIVERSITY BY FIVE-YEAR AGE GROUPS 15-75+, SAMOA

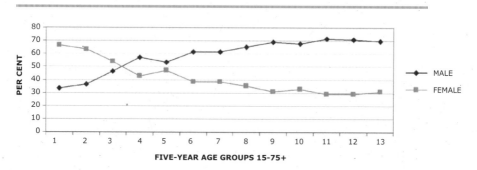

FIVE-YEAR AGE GROUPS 15-75+

*Source: Government of Samoa, 2003c.*

While there have been positive developments in post-school education and training, the numbers of enrolments are still insignificant against the number not enrolled. In 2001 the total population between the ages of 15-25 was 34,503 and the average number in each age cohort in that range was 3,137 with none less than 2,614. The majority of any age cohort are outside formal tertiary education. This group should not be seen as 'drop outs' as the vast majority will be engaged in economically and socially worthwhile activities. However, they are outside the formal track of educational provision and as a consequence do not have easy access to up-grading of skills. Establishing a meaningful national strategy for the post-school sector requires that the scope of the issue must be recognised. In fact, constant pressure on the formal post-school institutions by increased numbers of applicants has pushed entry standards up. The paradox that is facing the national system is that with a chronic skills shortage in all areas, access to technical and vocational education has to be rationed and entry standards to post-school higher education are being raised (Government of Samoa, 2005c).

In terms of employment, we see a very different picture, with more than twice as many males employed as females. Table 20 shows the disaggregation of employment by industry and gender. The figures show that the bulk of employment is within the 'agriculture, hunting and forestry' and 'manufacturing in traditional/ home setting' categories (41 per cent). The majority of males are involved in agriculture, hunting and forestry, while the greatest numbers of females are also concentrated in this sector as well as manufacturing in traditional/ home setting. Females outnumber males in home and service related activities such as manufacturing in traditional/ home setting; wholesale and retail trade; education; financing, insurance and business servicing; health and social work; international organisation; and also in manufacturing in formal setting where they may compromise the bulk of the process workers in enterprises such as Yazaki and Vailima.[18]

---

18   Yazaki International is a Japanese company that constructed a wire-harnessing plant in 1996 that has become the country's biggest private sector employer. Vailima Breweries produce and export beer.

TABLE 20: DISTRIBUTION OF EMPLOYMENT BY INDUSTRY, 2001, SAMOA

| | TOTAL | % | MALE | % | FEMALE | % |
|---|---|---|---|---|---|---|
| AGRICULTURE, HUNTING, FORESTRY | 17,711 | 35 | 15,613 | 44 | 2,098 | 14 |
| MANUFACTURING IN TRADITIONAL/ HOME SETTING | 5,422 | 11 | 1,912 | 5 | 3,510 | 23 |
| PUBLIC ADMINISTRATION | 3,322 | 7 | 2,143 | 6 | 1,179 | 8 |
| PRIVATE HOUSEHOLD WITH EMPLOYEES | 2,884 | 6 | 2,022 | 6 | 862 | 6 |
| WHOLESALE AND RETAIL TRADE | 2,757 | 5 | 1,460 | 4 | 1,297 | 9 |
| FISHING ACTIVITIES | 2,575 | 5 | 2,240 | 6 | 335 | 2 |
| EDUCATION | 2,341 | 5 | 864 | 2 | 1,477 | 10 |
| OTHER COMMUNITY, SOCIAL AND PERSONAL SERVICES | 2,096 | 4 | 1,566 | 4 | 530 | 3 |
| MANUFACTURING IN FORMAL SETTING | 1,941 | 4 | 907 | 3 | 1,034 | 7 |
| TRANSPORT, STORAGE AND COMMUNICATION | 1,929 | 4 | 1,636 | 5 | 293 | 2 |
| CONSTRUCTION | 1,674 | 3 | 1,601 | 5 | 73 | 0 |
| RESTAURANTS AND HOTELS | 1,522 | 3 | 770 | 2 | 752 | 5 |
| FINANCING, INSURANCE AND BUSINESS SERVICING | 1,082 | 2 | 526 | 1 | 556 | 4 |
| ELECTRICITY, GAS AND WATER | 906 | 2 | 808 | 2 | 98 | 1 |
| HEALTH AND SOCIAL WORK | 843 | 2 | 341 | 1 | 502 | 3 |
| INTERNATIONAL ORGANISATION | 472 | 1 | 220 | 1 | 252 | 2 |
| REAL ESTATE, RENTING AND BUSINESS SERVICES | 268 | 1 | 175 | 0 | 93 | 1 |
| NOT STATED | 854 | 2 | 545 | 2 | 309 | 2 |
| TOTAL | 50,599 | 100 | 35,349 | 100 | 15,250 | 100 |

Source: Government of Samoa, 2003c.

The 2001 census indicated that about 50 per cent of the population aged 15 years and over were economically active (52,998 persons). Two thirds of the economically active population was male (36,772). About 25 per cent of the population worked in a paid job and another 25 per cent worked in agriculture. However, the census reports that while there are fewer females in work than males, females had a lower proportion of unpaid work than their male counterparts, indicating that females who did become economically active were more likely to choose and gain paid employment than males. These statistics allow us to surmise that, other than those who attend the already-mentioned alternative education centres that take in boys who have dropped out from the secondary education system, boys leaving education will enter some form of economic activity, but this could often be within the informal or traditional agricultural sectors that do not always guarantee regular pay.

# CULTURAL CONTEXT: MASCULINITY, GENDER IDENTITY AND SOCIETAL RESPONSIBILITY

The Samoan culture has a complex construction of male gender identity and masculinity that is intrinsically connected to strong societal responsibility for the family and the collective. The culture is based on a *fa'amatai*, a system of village government by chiefs called *matais*. The *matai* governs an entire *aiga* or extended family. The *aiga* is the foundation of the wider society. Boys in particular are encouraged to respect the *matai*, and young men will see that the greatest honour is to become *matai* but know this is only achieved by visible evidence of support to community welfare.

*The Samoan culture has a complex construction of male gender identity and masculinity that is intrinsically connected to strong societal responsibility for the family and the collective.*

The relationship of brothers (all male relatives) to sisters (all female relatives) is defined in terms of a protectorship, where the brother is the provider and protector of the sister. Once children are old enough to work, their relationship to their parents becomes that of caregiver and service provider in return for the years they had been taken care of. The relationship of extended families within a village is defined by the hierarchy of high chiefs and orators. Together, the village families operate as kinsfolk bound by a common heritage as signalled by the village honorific.

Gender-specific roles are followed. Girls are expected to be competent in the women's tasks of weaving and the like. The young women enter the *aualuma* or village women's committee, which focuses on the production of traditional mats and the welfare of the families. The young men enter the *aumaga* or men's group and focus on developing proficiency in fishing, agricultural tasks, food preparation and the *'ava* ceremony (held on special occasions). Leadership is held by the chiefs and orators in a mutually dependent relationship. In everything, people operate as kinsfolk in the activities that sustain their lives in the village.

The link to walkabout and other rites of passage is through a system of what can most simply be called community service. The so-called 'untitled men' (*taulelea*) are the strength of the village and its workforce: the farmers, the fisherman and, in former times, the warriors. They remain untitled until such time as they are chosen by the family to be a *matai*. Service is a significant factor in choosing a *matai* as expressed in the Samoan saying: *"O le ala I le pule o le tautua"* (the way to authority is through service).

There is a sophisticated hierarchy when it comes to the views of youth reaching the ears of the village council. They have a choice of three avenues: *aualuma* – the female descendents of the village, *aiga* – their family or *aumaga* – the group of untitled men. Views have to be filtered through these gate-keepers before they reach the council of chiefs. The village council still has remarkable power, but this is increasingly coming into conflict with movements away from traditional society as the country becomes modernised. The implications of this could result in alienation and social disenfranchisement for boys and adolescents. A worrying factor within Samoan society is the high incidence of suicide among males. Table 21 shows the suicide numbers since 2000 disaggregated by sex. Over these six years, three quarters of suicides were males. The age range for males was from 10 to 76 years old. It is possible, though difficult to prove, that there is a link between boys' underachievement in education, the suicide rates and the traditional system of administration. More research is needed into these aspects to understand the association and linkages.

TABLE 21: SUICIDE NUMBERS BY SEX, 2000-2005, SAMOA

|  | 2000 | 2001 | 2002 | 2003 | 2004 | 2005 | TOTAL | % |
|---|---|---|---|---|---|---|---|---|
| MALE | 11 | 11 | 7 | 8 | 16 | 5 | 58 | 75 |
| FEMALE | 3 | 4 | 2 | 4 | 3 | 1 | 17 | 22 |
| NOT KNOWN | 1 | 1 |  |  |  |  | 2 | 3 |
| TOTALS | 15 | 16 | 9 | 12 | 19 | 6 | 77 | 100 |

*Source: Fa'ataua le Ola, 2005.*

# DON BOSCO TECHNICAL CENTRE

## Background

Don Bosco Technical Centre is a single-sex institution that responds to the needs of marginalised boys who left regular formal secondary schools without completing the course. The Centre aims to facilitate holistic development of boys through focusing on technology education, career preparation and opportunities to develop social awareness. It opened with 32 students in 1989 and the number had increased to 250 in 2005. Students are mainly from the rural villages of the two largest islands, Upolu and Savaii.

The Centre provides a four-year programme of study in design and technology associated with woodwork, metalwork, plumbing, mechanical engineering and boat building. The contents include theory, practical applications and information about the range of available career possibilities. In addition, students are offered courses in mathematics, communication skills, *fa'asamoa*[19] or cultural education, basic literacy and religious education. The Centre also seeks to develop in its students the virtues of honesty, integrity, responsibility, trust and loyalty and strives to foster a commitment towards religious and moral convictions.

The Centre operates a flexible arrangement whereby students may leave on finding employment. Students who remain at the Centre for the full four years have a very high rate of success in terms of finding work or continuing with their studies. The curriculum is aimed at preparing students for employment, self-employment or to go on to further studies at Samoa Polytechnic. This case study is a brief investigation into the philosophy and practices of the institution in relation to the educational development of boys.

## Boys' experience of barriers to achievement in mainstream schools

Eleven groups of factors were identified by students as barriers to their achievement in mainstream schools. In order of the most frequently to the least frequently mentioned, these were:

1   teacher and teaching-related factors,

2   home factors,

---

19   *Fa'asamoa* refers to the Samoan way of life and encompasses beliefs, values and cultural practices.

3  poor self-image and behaviour,

4  girl-related factors,

5  school rules and punishment,

6  language and literacy,

7  drugs,

8  peer pressure,

9  school management,

10 attitudes and behaviour of others, and

11 resources.

*Teachers' attitudes appeared to be a major issue in underachievement as students experienced disrespect in the form of corporal punishment, threatening language, humiliation, favouritism and lack of attention to weak students.*

Teachers' attitudes appeared to be a major issue in underachievement as students experienced disrespect in the form of corporal punishment, threatening language, humiliation, favouritism and lack of attention to weak students. Pedagogy was described as narrow, uninspiring, not providing feedback or review and not providing differential learning for varying abilities. The most frequently identified home factor was poverty in terms of being cash-poor, resulting in an inability to pay school fees and meet other school costs. The presence of girls was viewed as distracting, and also leading to fear of being ridiculed in front of them. Interestingly, none of the students mentioned any alienation from school as a result of perceptions that school or academic achievement is a 'feminine' pursuit or pastime, a factor that has come up in studies on boys' achievement in countries such as Australia and Jamaica. It appears that poor performance also emanates from poor knowledge of English, which is the medium of instruction in secondary schools. A test of students entering the Centre showed that none of them had the proficiency required for learning other subjects through that language.

## Aspirations and achievements at the Centre

Students at Don Bosco Technical Centre were mostly aspiring to have the requisite skills for finding a livelihood option. A strong sense of wanting to pay back a debt to parents, church and society exists. Boys seem to bear on their shoulders the burden of being the breadwinner and protector. Students reported a sense of achievement at the Centre in terms of the enhancement of skills related to technology and its application and the development of appropriate attitudes, values and behaviour, and other life skills. Many of them also reported improvement in language skills. They acknowledged developing a sense of purposefulness, a keenness to learn and a disciplined lifestyle. They also made special mention of communication skills in which many spoke of an increased confidence to interact in group, class and whole school situations with audiences of different ages. The boys also appreciated the emphasis on developing independence and self-confidence shown in letting them design and complete projects on their own. Students felt respected and cared for.

Students were clearly positive in their sense of belonging to the Centre. They enjoyed going to school and felt engaged in the activities. They experienced and appreciated the sense of purposefulness, and showed a keenness to learn and a disciplined lifestyle. Many of them felt that the Centre had contributed in bringing positive changes to their outlook and behaviour. There was a sense of pride in what they had been able to achieve. Therefore, an important part of their achievements at Don Bosco was regaining their sense of self, a desire to try harder, be productive and make a contribution to family and village, and to seek further knowledge and understanding in order to achieve all this. Learning life skills was highlighted by students as an important accomplishment, and they acknowledged achievements in religious knowledge and application.

One source of pride has come from the emphasis on knowledge, skills and values associated with racing the long boats or *fautasi*. These were the traditional means of transport between islands or around the coastal villages of the same island. They each have around 50 rowers and are now primarily used in competitions during national celebrations. Besides Don Bosco, no other school has rowed a *fautasi* during the national competitions. Rowing was also used as an opportunity to teach science and cultural principles involved in boat design, the art and skills of rowing, the discipline involved in maintaining fitness, and the principles of working as a team and making monetary contribution to the school through their prize money.

## Effective approaches and processes at the Centre

Analysis of the processes at the Centre led to the identification of seven principles that helped in achieving high levels of acceptance and support from students and ensured their good performance. These principles were identified by the students themselves in the order that they are presented:

1 enabling school environment,

2 school leadership, attitudes and philosophy,

3 nature of the curriculum,

4 education for life,

5 teachers' attitudes and philosophy,

6 teachers' pedagogical knowledge and skills, and

7 teacher-student relationship.

The school emphasises creating space for respectful and meaningful dialogue between teachers and students, principal and students, and students and students. An annual retreat organised as a residential one-week event for the entire school provides an excellent opportunity for team-building. Regular whole school meetings with the principal are another method for developing a shared vision and sense of ownership. The principal used these meetings to challenge, motivate and counsel the students, and they are perceived by students as having a great impact. The Centre's participation in outside-school events – including competing in the *fautasi* races, performing traditional dances and having sports teams in the local competitions during national celebrations – helps in developing a collective identity and cooperative attitude. Highlighting the achievement of students is followed as a strategy to build and nurture their self-esteem and self image. The school does not allow corporate punishment.

*The school emphasises creating space for respectful and meaningful dialogue between teachers and students, principal and students, and students and students.*

The combination of theory with practical and workplace experience is clearly considered an effective approach by both students and teachers. The incorporation of life skills, values and culture in planned curricular activities helps in giving education a lifelong focus. The development of interpersonal skills, understanding gender-related issues, diversity, decision-making skills, creative thinking and problem-solving skills, analytical skills for assessing self and others, information-gathering skills, and coping and stress-management skills prepare them to face the world for life. Teaching styles are such that they depict confidence in students' ability to do things on their own. Students appreciated teachers' special attention to those who were perceived to be weak. Teacher-student relationships appeared to be relaxed and based on trust and respect.

## Gender identity: notions of masculinity

It is interesting to note that the notion of masculinity promoted in the Centre matches that prevalent in traditional Samoan society. The boys most often see themselves in the role of protector of their parents, sisters, extended family, village and church. They see themselves as being responsible for providing for their food needs and shelter and meeting family obligations to the church and the village. The relationship to sisters is sacred and seen as *feagaiga* or covenant, the *i'oimata* or 'pupil of the brothers' eye'. This means as males their duties are to protect their sisters, be of service through ensuring there is sufficient food and that it is cooked for them, and do all the household chores. Although following patriarchy where women have limited economic and political rights, in Samoan society boys and men are expected to cook and do other work in the household. Masculinity is also associated with leadership for which, as noted earlier, service is a prerequisite. Through service, males can learn to be leaders responsible for safeguarding family assets, distributing family resources and representing the family at village and church forums.

There is a strong belief among the boys of this masculine identity being their heritage. The school also seems to reinforce these notions through "making the boys aware of their role in families and society; to become good fathers, *matai* and providers of the family", as expressed by one teacher. Notions of masculinity are grounded in cultural beliefs and practices that are very much part of life in their villages. This has helped in giving the boys a strong identity. However, it can be questioned on the ground that it does not help in any way in reducing some of the pressures on boys or some of the restrictions that girls face.

# CONCLUSIONS

The case study provides a number of signals for addressing the issue of boys' underachievement, though some of them remain inconclusive and others need careful interpretation. The positive experiences of students at Don Bosco Technical Centre clearly indicate the need for reforming the school pedagogy, management processes and teachers in terms of their attitude and approach. This indication is quite definitive and it is also clear how the contrasts in such experiences between mainstream secondary school and this Centre had helped students gain confidence and feelings of self-worth. Another important issue relates to the issue of vocationalisation. Such positive experiences are often taken as an indicator of the need for the secondary level of education to be vocationalised, especially for boys. While there is no doubt that some of the vocational courses need to be incorporated as a choice available to students, this cannot be promoted as the most desirable option for boys, especially those coming from rural or lower socio-economic backgrounds. What can be said here with greater confidence is that some of the processes and approaches used for vocational courses at the Centre provide principles for making any classroom pedagogy more interesting and effective. This includes the focus on interactive activities, showing confidence in students by allowing them handle complete projects themselves, and so on.

*...some of the processes and approaches used for vocational courses at the Centre provide principles for making any classroom pedagogy more interesting and effective. This includes the focus on interactive activities...*

The case study does not provide definite indicators regarding single-sex school. Although the absence of girls appeared to have helped the boys, the presence of girls did not emerge as the most important reason for low performance in mainstream secondary schools. Another critical area is notions about maleness, masculinity and boys' ability to process themselves as males in Samoa, and the interactions between these philosophies, practices and some of the evident patterns for males such as suicide and underachievement. As noted earlier, the overwhelming majority of those who commit suicide are males, and with such deep-rooted beliefs in the role of the male in servitude to the family, it would be important to find out what happens to male's notions of dignity when they find themselves in positions of underachievement at school and then in the community if they are unable to get paid employment. In sum, this being the first study in Samoa focusing on boys' educational achievement, there are many unknown areas that should be the focus of future research.

# bibliography

Abagi O (2003). "The Report of Gender Audit in the Education Sector". Maseru: Ministry of Education and Training (unpublished consultancy report).

Asian Development Bank (ADB) (2003). *Samoa: Country Strategy and Program Update (2004-2006)*. Apia: ADB Samoa Country Programme.

Aitken, Judith (1999). "The Achievement of Boys". New Zealand: Education Review Office. *www.ero.govt.nz*.

Alloway, N, P Freebody, P Gilbert and S Muspratt (2002). *Boys, Literacy and Schooling: Expanding the Repertoires of Practice*. Canberra: Commonwealth Department of Education, Science and Training.

Australian Bureau of Statistics (2005). "Australian Social Trends: School Students' Mathematics and Science Literacy". Available as 4102.0 at *www.abs.gov.au/*.

Australian Council for Educational Research (ACER) and OECD (2001). *PISA in Brief from Australia's Perspective: Highlights from the Full Australian Report*. Camberwell: ACER. Available at *www.ozpisa.acer.edu.au/reports.html*.

Australian Government, Department of Education, Science and Training (2003). "Meeting the challenge: Guiding principles for success from the Boys' Education Lighthouse Schools (BELS) Programme Stage One 2003". Canberra: Commonwealth of Australia. Available at *www.dest.gov.au/sectors/school_education/ publications_resources/profiles/meeting_the_challenge_final_report.htm*.

Australian Government, Department of Education, Science and Training (2005a). "Boys' Education Lighthouse Schools (BELS) Stage Two". Canberra: Commonwealth of Australia. Available at *www.dest.gov.au/sectors/school_education/publications_resources/ profiles/boys_education_lighthouse_schools_bels_stage_two.htm*.

Australian Government, Department of Education, Science and Training (2005b). "Boys' Education Lighthouse Schools". Canberra: Commonwealth of Australia. Available at *www.dest.gov.au/sectors/school_education/policy_initiatives_reviews/key_issues/boys_ education/bels.htm*.

Australian Government, Department of Education, Science and Training (2005c). "Success for Boys". Canberra: Commonwealth of Australia. Available at *www. dest.gov.au/sectors/school_education/policy_initiatives_reviews/key_issues/boys_education/ success_for_boys.htm*.

Bailey, B and M Bernard (2003). "Establishing a Database of Gender Differentials in Enrolment and Performance at the Secondary and Tertiary Levels of the Caribbean Education Systems". The Canada-Caribbean Gender Equality Fund Programme II, CARICOM.

Baksh-Soodeen, Rawwida (2003). "Gender, Boys and Education". In *Commonwealth Education Partnerships 2003*. London: The Stationary Office.

Bress, P (2000). "Gender Differences in Teaching Styles". *English-Teaching Forum*, 38(4), October.

*Boys in Schools Bulletin* (2000a). "Indigenous Education Workers Talk about Boys". *Boys in Schools Bulletin*, 3(4).

*Boys in Schools Bulletin* (2000b). "Evidence from 'across the ditch': New Zealand research on boys in schools". *Boys in Schools Bulletin*, 3(1).

Brown, J (2001) "Boys in (and out of) School in Jamaica". *Boys in Schools Bulletin*, 4(3).

Challender, C (2004) "Natural Resources: From Curse to Blessing". *Equals Newsletter* (Beyond Access: Gender, Education and Development), Issue 4, January.

Coard, B (1971). *How the West Indian Child is Made Educationally Subnormal in the British School System*. London: New Beacon Books

Cohen, L (2004). "From strength to strength: A Lighthouse case study from the West Wallsend cluster, NSW." *Boys in Schools Bulletin*, 7(1): 38-43.

Collins, C, J Kenway and J McLeod (2000). "Factors influencing the educational performance of males and females in school and their initial destinations after leaving school". Canberra: Commonwealth of Australia Department of Education, Training and Youth Affairs.

Connell R W (1987). *Gender and Power*. Cambridge: Polity.

Connell, R W (1996). "Teaching the boys: New research on masculinity, and gender studies for schools". *Teachers College Record*, 98(2): 206-235.

Crotty, M (2001). *Making the Australian Male: Middle-Class Masculinity, 1870-1920*. Melbourne: Melbourne University Press.

Davis, J ( 2002) "Boys to Men: Masculine Diversity and Schooling". Paper presented at the School Leadership Centre of Trinidad and Tobago.

De Bortoli, Lisa and John Cresswell (2004). "Australia's Indigenous Students in PISA 2000: Results from an International Study". ACER Research Monograph No 59. Camberwell: Australian Council for Educational Research. Available at *www.acer.edu.au*.

Dodds, Tony (2003). "From government correspondence schools to parastatal colleges of open learning: out-of-school secondary education at a distance in central and southern Africa". In Jo Bradley (Ed), *The Open Classroom: Distance Learning in and out of Schools*. London: Kogan Page Limited.

Dunne, M et al (2005). "Gendered School Experiences: The Impact of Retention and Achievement in Botswana and Ghana". *Researching the Issues*, 56. Department for International Development (DFID).

Epstein, D (1998) "Real boys don't work: 'underachievement', masculinity, and the harassment of 'sissies'". In D Epstein et al (Eds), *Failing Boys? Issues in Gender and Achievement*. Buckingham: Open University Press.

Epstein, D, J Elwood, V Hey and J Maw (1998). "Schoolboy frictions: feminism and 'failing' boys". In D Epstein et al (Eds), *Failing Boys? Issues in Gender and Achievement*. Buckingham: Open University Press.

Evans, H (1999). "Gender and achievement in secondary education in Jamaica". Working Paper 2. Kingston: Planning Institute of Jamaica, Policy Development Unit, Social Policy Analysis and Research Project.

Fa'ataua le Ola (2005). A report by the NGO on suicide in Samoa.

Figueroa, M (2000). "Making Sense of the Male Experience: The Case of Academic Underachievement in the English-Speaking Caribbean". *IDS Bulletin*, 31(2).

Foster, V, M Kimmel and C Skelton (2001). "'What about the boys?' An overview of the debates". In W Martino and B Meyenn (Eds), *What about the boys? Issues of masculinity in schools*. Buckingham: Open University Press.

Gibson, T and L Martinez (2003). "Boys: getting it right?" *Redress: Journal of the Association of Women Educators*, 12(1): 15-17.

Gifford, M (2003a). "Boys in schools programme: rock and water". Newcastle, Australia: University of Newcastle. Available at *www.newcastle.edu.au/centre/fac/binsp/programs/rockandwater/*.

Gifford, M and D Hartman (2003). "BEBOP: Boys' Education Boys' Outcomes Project". *Boys in Schools Bulletin*, 6(1): 16-19.

Gilbert, P and R Gilbert (2001). "Masculinity, inequality and post-school opportunities: disrupting oppositional politics about boys' education". *International Journal of Inclusive Education* 5(1): 1-13.

Gilbert, R and P Gilbert (1998). *Masculinity Goes to School*. London: Routledge.

Gorard, S, J Salisbury and G Rees (1999). "Revisiting the apparent underachievement of boys: reflections on the implications for educational research". Paper presented at the British Educational Research Association Annual Conference, University of Sussex at Brighton, 2-5 September.

Government of Lesotho and the World Bank (2005). "Policy, Planning and Management of Teachers in Lesotho". Available at *www.ilo.org/public/english/dialogue/sector/ap/educat/forums/docs/pretoria-lesotho-report.pdf*.

Government of Samoa (1995a). *Western Samoa Education Policies 1995-2005*. Apia: Department of Education.

Government of Samoa (1995b). *Western Samoa Education Strategies 1995-2005*. Apia: Department of Education.

Government of Samoa (1996). *Statement of Economic Strategy, A New Partnership 1996-1997*. Apia: Government of Samoa.

Government of Samoa. (2001a). *2000 Labour Market Survey of Private Sector Employers in Samoa: Market Appraisal of Livelihood Opportunities Project*. Apia, Department of Labour.

Government of Samoa (2001b). *Towards an Urban Planning and Management Strategy for Apia, Samoa*. Apia: Government of Samoa and Asian Development Bank Technical Assistance Project.

Government of Samoa (2001c). *Analytical Paper: Student Outcomes by Gender in Examination Results 2001*. Apia: Department of Education Policy, Planning and Research Division.

Government of Samoa (2002a). *2001 Labour Market Survey of Semi Formal Sector in Samoa Market Appraisal of Livelihood Opportunities Project*. Apia: Department of Labour.

Government of Samoa (2002b). *Statistical Digest 2002*. Apia: Department of Education.

Government of Samoa (2002c). *Strategy for the Development of Samoa 2002-2004*. Apia: Economic Policy and Planning Division, Ministry of Finance.

Government of Samoa (2003a). *Annual Abstract 2001–2002*. Apia: Division of Statistical Services.

Government of Samoa (2003b). *Annual Statistical Abstract 2001-2002*. Apia: Division of Statistical Services.

Government of Samoa (2003c). *Report of the Census of Population and Housing 2001*. Apia: Division of Statistical Services.

Government of Samoa (2004a). *Educational Statistical Digest*. Apia: Ministry of Education, Sports and Culture.

Government of Samoa (2004b). *Ministry of Women, Community and Social Development Corporate Plan 2004-2007*. Apia: Ministry of Women, Community and Social Development.

Government of Samoa (2004c). "Samoa Education Sector Project II Draft Education Sector Review. September 2004". Apia: Ministry of Education, Sports and Culture, prepared by Helinski Consulting Group and ANZEC Limited.

Government of Samoa (2005a). "Non-formal education in Samoa: Report of the research". Draft, 9 September. Apia: Ministry of Education, Sports and Culture

Government of Samoa (2005b). "Samoa Education Sector Evaluation Study. Draft Report and Recommendations. 9 September 2005". Apia: Ministry of Education, Sports and Culture. Prepared by PRIDE Project.

Government of Samoa (2005c). *Educational Statistical Digest 2005, Part II*. Apia: Ministry of Education, Sports and Culture.

Government of Samoa (2005d). *Strategy for the Development of Samoa 2005–2007*. Apia: Economic Policy and Planning Division, Ministry of Finance.

Government of Samoa (2005e). *Educational Statistical Digest*. Apia: Ministry of Education, Sports and Culture.

Graham, M and G Robinson (2004). "'The Silent Catastrophe': Institutional Racism in the British Educational System and the Underachievement of Black Boys". *Journal of Black Studies*, 34, Part 5.

Green, Lyndsay and Lawry Trevor-Deutsch (2002). *Women and ICTs for Open and Distance Learning: Some Experiences and Strategies from the Commonwealth*. Vancouver: Commonwealth of Learning.

Harrison, S (2002). "Engaging boys in the arts". Paper presented at the Australian Association for Research in Education annual conference, Brisbane.

Hayes, D and B Lingard (2003). "Introduction: rearticulating gender agendas in schooling: an Australian.perspective". *International Journal of Inclusive Education*, 7(1): 1-6.

Hayes, D, M Mills, P Christie and B Lingard (in press). *Teachers making a Difference: Productive pedagogies, assessment and performance*. Sydney: Allen & Unwin.

Hickey, C. (2003). "What is it about boys? Adding fuel to an ongoing debate". *Independent Education*, 33(11-12).

House of Representatives, Standing Committee on Education and Training (2002). "Boys: getting it right: report on the inquiry into the education of boys". Canberra: Commonwealth of Australia. Available at *www.aph.gov.au/house/committee/edt/eofb/report/fullrpt.pdf*).

Hunte, K (2002). "Gender Equality, Male Under-Achievement". *MOE Insight*, Ministry of Education, Guyana. Available at *www.education.gov.gy*.

Itano, Nicole (2004). "In Lesotho, boys go to farm while girls hit the books". *The Christian Science Monitor*, 27 July.

Jackson, D (1998). "Breaking out of the binary trap: Boys' underachievement, schooling and gender relations". In D Epstein et al (Eds), *Failing Boys? Issues in Gender and Achievement*. Buckingham: Open University Press.

Jenkins, Janet (1993). "Distance Education for Small Countries". In Kevin M Lillis (Ed), *Policy, Planning and Management of Education in Small States*. Paris: UNESCO/ International Institute for Educational Planning. Available at *www1.worldbank.org/ disted/Management/Governance/iss-02.html*.

Jobo, M et al (2001). "Lesotho: A Baseline Study of the Teacher Education System". Multi-Site Teacher Education Research Project (MUSTER), Discussion Paper 8. Centre for International Education, University of Sussex.

Jones, S and D Myhill (2004a). "Seeing Things Differently: Boys as Underachievers". *Gender and Education*, 16(4).

Jones, S and D Myhill (2004b). "'Troublesome boys' and 'compliant girls': Gender identity and perceptions of achievement and underachievement". *British Journal of Sociology of Education*, 25(5).

Keddie, A (2004). "Working with boys' peer cultures: Productive Pedagogies... productive boys". *Curriculum Perspectives*, 24(1): 20-29.

Keddie, A (2005). "A framework for best practice in boys' education: key requisite knowledges and Productive Pedagogies". *Pedagogy, Culture and Society*, 13(1): 59-74.

Kenway, J (1997). Boys' education, masculinity and gender reform: some introductory remarks. In J Kenway (Ed), *Will boys be boys?: Boys' education in the context of gender reform*. Deakin West: Australian Curriculum Studies Association.

Kenway, J and S Willis with J Blackmore and L Rennie (1997). *Answering back: girls, boys and feminism in schools*. Sydney: Allen & Unwin.

Kimane, I, M Ntimo-Makara and M Molise (1998). "The Socio-Cultural Context of Basotho: Towards Informed Population and Development Planning in the Next Millenium – Draft Report of the Study Conducted on Behalf of the Department of Population and Manpower Planning, Ministry of Planning, Government of Lesotho with Support from UNFPA". Maseru: Ministry of Planning (unpublished consultancy report).

Lingard, B (1998). "Contextualising and utilising the 'what about the boys?' backlash for gender equity goals". *Change: Transformations in Education*, 1(2): 16-30.

Lingard, B (2003). "Where to in gender theorising and policy after recuperative masculinity politics?" *International Journal of Inclusive Education*, 7(1): 33-56.

Lingard, B and P Douglas (1999). *Men engaging feminisms: pro-feminism, backlashes and schooling*. Buckingham: Open University Press.

Lingard, B, W Martino, M Mills and M Bahr (2002). "Addressing the educational needs of boys". Canberra: Australian Government, Department of Education, Science and Training.

Ludowyke, J (2002). "Directing change: national enquiry into boys' education". *AEU (SA Branch) Journal*, 34(2): 9, 15.

Mahoney, P (1998). "Girls will be girls and boys will be first". In D Epstein et al (Eds), *Failing Boys? Issues in Gender and Achievement*. Buckingham: Open University Press.

Ma'ia'i, F (1957). "A Study of the Developing Pattern of Education and the Factors Influencing that Development in New Zealand's Pacific Dependencies". *Education*. Wellington, NZ: Victoria University of Wellington: 395.

Makhetha, L and S Motlomelo (2004). "The Evaluation of the Learning Post Programme (LPP) Pilot Project for the Non-Formal Education Unit". Maseru: Ministry of Education and Training and the NUL Institute of Education (unpublished report).

Marks, J (2001). *Girls Know Better: Educational Attainment of Boys and Girls*. London: CIVITAS – the Institute for the Study of Civil Society.

Martino, W and D Berrill (2003). "Boys, schooling and masculinities: interrogating the 'right' way to educate boys". *Educational Review*, 55(2): 99-117.

Martino, W and B Meyenn (Eds) (2001). *What about the boys? Issues of masculinity and schooling*. Buckingham: Open University Press.

Martino, W and M Pallotta-Chiarolli (2001). *Boys' stuff: boys talking about what matters*. Sydney: Allen & Unwin.

Martino, W and M Pallotta-Chiarolli (2003). *So what's a boy? Addressing issues of masculinity and schooling*. Crow's Nest: Allen & Unwin.

McNamara, F (2002). "Boys: getting some of it right". *Professional Magazine*, 19: 8-9.

Mills, M (1997). "Implementing boys' programs in schools: debates and dilemmas". Paper presented at the Australian Association for Research in Education annual conference, Brisbane.

Mills, M (2000a). "Issues in implementing boys' programmes in schools: male teachers and empowerment". *Gender and Education*, 12(2): 221-238.

Mills, M (2000b). "Troubling the 'failing boys' discourse". *Discourse: studies in the cultural politics of education*, 21(2): 237-246.

Mills, M (2001). *Challenging violence in schools: an issue of masculinities*. Buckingham: Open University Press.

Mokhosi, E B, M Shale, M Molapo and J O Jegede (1999). "The Situational and Needs Analysis Survey of Herdboys in Lesotho". Maseru: UNICEF and NUL-CONSULS (unpublished research report).

Mortimore, P, P Sammons, L Stoll, D Lewis and R Ecob (1988). *School Matters: The Junior Years*. Somerset: Open Books Publishing.

Mukhopadhyay, Marmar and Susan Phillips (Eds) (1994). *Open Schooling: Selected Experiences*. Vancouver: Commonwealth of Learning.

Nelson, B (2003). Foreword to "Meeting the challenge: summary report – guiding principles for success from the Boys' Education Lighthouse Schools Programme Stage One 2003". Canberra: Australian Government, Department of Education, Science and Training.

Nyland, B (2001). "Language, literacy and participation rights: Factors influencing educational outcomes for Australian boys". Paper prepared for the AARE Conference in Fremantle, December.

OFSTED (1996). *The Gender Divide: Performance Differences Between Boys and Girls at School*. London: Office for Standards in Education and Equal Opportunities Commission.

Parry, O (1998). "Boys will be boys – why Caribbean males underachieve". In R Reddock (Ed), *Construction of Caribbean Masculinity*. Jamaica: University of the West Indies Press.

Plummer, David (1999). *One of the Boys: Masculinity, Homophobia and Modern Manhood*. New York: Haworth Press

Plummer, David (2003). "Homophobia". In Michael Kimmel and Amy Aronson (Eds), *Men and Masculinities: A social, cultural and historical encyclopedia*. Santa Barbara, CA: ABC-Clio Press.

Plummer, David (2005). "Crimes against manhood: Homophobia as the penalty for betraying hegemonic masculinity". In G Hawkes and J Scott (Eds), *Perspectives in Human Sexuality*. Melbourne: Oxford University Press.

Policy Analysis, Research and Statistics Unit (2006). Planning and Development Division, Ministry of Education and Youth, Jamaica, 30 May.

PPSEAWA (Women for Peace, Understanding and Advancement, Inclusion International, National Council of Women (NCW) and members of Civil Society) (2004). "NGO Shadow Report on The Status of Women in Samoa". Samoa Umbrella for Non-Government Organizations (SUNGO), December. Available at *www.iwraw-ap.org/resources/shadow_reports.htm*.

Proudford, C (1999). "Programs for boys: penetrating emotional barriers". Paper presented at the Australian Association for Research in Education annual conference, Melbourne.

Reed, L R (1998). "'Zero tolerance': gender performance and school failure". In D Epstein et al (Eds), *Failing Boys? Issues in Gender and Achievement*. Buckingham: Open University Press.

Report of Education Scrutiny Panel (2003). "Under-achievement of Turkish-Speaking Boys". London Borough of Hackney.

Richardson, B (Ed) (2005). *Tell it Like it is: How Our Schools Fail Black Children*. London: Bookmarks Publications and Trentham Books.

Roulston, K and M Mills (2000). "Male teachers in feminised teaching areas: Marching to the beat of the men's movement drums?" *Oxford Review of Education*, 26(2): 221-237.

Sewell, T (1998). "Loose canons: exploding the myth of the 'black macho' lad". In D Epstein et al (Eds), *Failing Boys? Issues in Gender and Achievement*. Buckingham: Open University Press.

Sewell, Tony and Barry Chevannes (2002). 'Emerging Masculinities: A Study of the Change From Within Methodology'. Unpublished Report. University of the West Indies and University of Leeds.

Slamet, D (2003). "The gender balance". *Australian Educator*, 38: 28-31.

Smithers, R (2005). "More help for underachieving black pupils". *The Guardian*, Friday 7 October.

State of New South Wales, The (2003). "Quality teaching in NSW public schools". Sydney: The State of New South Wales, Department of Education and Training. Available at: *www.curriculumsupport.nsw.edu.au/qualityTeaching/docs/QualityTeachEPSColor.pdf*.

State of Queensland, The (2001). "The Queensland school reform longitudinal study (QSRLS)". Brisbane: The State of Queensland, Department of Education.

State of Queensland, The (2004). "The New Basics Project". Brisbane: The State of Queensland Department of Education and the Arts. Available at: *http://education.qld.gov.au/corporate/newbasics/*.

Telefoni, H M (2003). "Government of Samoa 2003/2004 Budget Address". Apia: Government of Samoa.

Thomson, Sue, John Cresswell and Lisa De Bortoli (2003). *Facing the Future: A Focus on Mathematical Literacy among Australian 15-year-old Students in PISA 2003*. Camberwell: ACER. Available at *www.ozpisa.acer.edu.au/reports.html*.

Tizard, B et al (1988). *Young Children at School in the Inner City*. Hove and London: Lawrence Erlbaum Associates.

Townsend, G (2003). "A class of their own". *Educare News*, 133: 22-24.

UNDP (2003). *Human Development Report 2003: Millennium Development Goals: A compact among nations to end human poverty*. New York: Oxford University Press.

UNDP (2005). *Human Development Report 2005: International cooperation at a crossroads: Aid, trade and security in an unequal world*. New York: Oxford University Press.

UNESCO (2004). *EFA Global Monitoring Report 2005: The Quality Imperative*. Paris: UNESCO.

UNESCO (2005). *EFA Global Monitoring Report 2006: Literacy for Life*. Paris: UNESCO.

UNICEF (2003). "Evaluation of the Alternative Learning Opportunities Programme". Maseru: UNICEF.

UNICEF (2004). "What about the Boys?" *In The State of the World's Children 2004*. New York: UNICEF.

Watson, T (2004). "Barnsley boys breaking through: BEBOP brings real behavioural changes". *Boys in Schools Bulletin*, 7(2): 31-33.

Weaver-Hightower, M (2003a). "Crossing the divide: Bridging the disjunctures between theoretically oriented and practice-oriented literature about masculinity and boys at school". *Gender and Education*, 15(4): 407-423.

Weaver-Hightower, M (2003b). "The 'boy turn' in research on gender and education". *Review of Educational Research*, 73(4): 471-498.

West, P (1999). "Boy's underachievement in school: Some persistent problems and some current research". *Issues in Educational Research*, 9(1).

West, P (2002). "'It ain't cool to like school': Why are boys underachieving around the world? And what can we do about it?" Available at *www.menshealth.uws.edu.au*.

Whitfield, G (2005). "Boys raise their game". *The Journal*, 7 October. Available at *www.icnewcastle.icnetwork.co.uk*

World Bank (2006). *World Development Report 2006*. Washington, DC: World Bank.

# about the authors

**Jyotsna Jha**, PhD in Economics of Education, works as Advisor, Education and Gender and Education and HIV/AIDS at the Commonwealth Secretariat in London. Prior to that she was based in India, where she had extensive experience in research, evaluation and implementation-support projects for both government and non-governmental organisations (NGOs), and for national and international agencies. Her previously published work includes a book titled *Elementary Education for the Poor and Other Deprived Groups: The Real Challenge of Universalisation* and chapters in *Gender and Social Policy in a Global Context* and *Reinventing Public Service Delivery in India: Selected Case Studies*. Most of her recent writing has focused on equity issues in education.

**Fatimah Kelleher** is a Programme Officer at the Commonwealth Secretariat and has been working on universal primary education (UPE), looking at such areas as education delivery to nomadic populations, teacher deployment, education sector planning and other factors surrounding the sustainability of UPE. She has previously worked with civil society, NGOs and government in Nigeria, Sudan and the UK, and has been involved with varied formal and informal programmes dealing with both education and gender issues.